Recipes from around the World

Everyday Cookbook

6/18

STAR
FIRE

Publisher and Creative Director: Nick Wells
Art Director: Mike Spender
Project Editor: Cat Emslie
Editorial Planning: Christian Anthony and Toria Lyle,
and Rosanna Singler (original edition)
Layout Design: Vanessa Green,
and Mike Spender and Colin Rudderham (original edition)
Digital Design and Production: Chris Herbert and Claire Walker

07 09 11 10 08

1 3 5 7 9 10 8 6 4 2

This edition first published in 2007 by
STAR FIRE
Crabtree Hall, Crabtree Lane,
Fulham, London, SW6 6TY
United Kingdom

www.star-fire.co.uk

STAR FIRE is part of The Foundry Creative Media Company Limited

© 2007 this edition The Foundry Creative Media Co. Ltd.

ISBN 978-1-84451-963-7

The CIP record for this book is available from the British Library.

Printed in China

Authors: Catherine Atkinson, Juliet Barker, Gina Steer, Vicki Smallwood,
Carol Tennant, Mari Mererid Williams, Elizabeth Wolf-Cohen and Simone Wright
Editorial (original edition): Sara Goulding and Sara Robson
Photography: Colin Bowling, Paul Forrester and Stephen Brayne
Home Economists and Stylists: Jacqueline Bellefontaine,
Mandy Phipps, Vicki Smallwood and Penny Stephens

All props supplied by Barbara Stewart at Surfaces

NOTE
Recipes using uncooked eggs should be avoided by infants,
the elderly, pregnant women and anyone suffering from an illness.

Contents

Soups & Starters

Light Bites

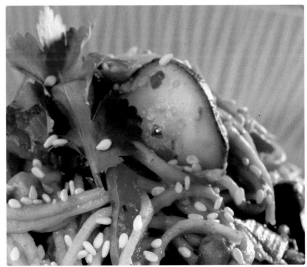

Main Meals

Desserts

Hygiene in the Kitchen

It is important to remember that many foods can carry some form of bacteria. In most cases, the worst it will lead to is a bout of food poisoning or gastroenteritis, although for certain people this can be serious. The risk can be reduced or eliminated, however, by good hygiene and proper cooking.

Do not buy food that is past its sell-by date and do not consume food that is past its use-by date. When buying food, use the eyes and nose. If the food looks tired, limp or a bad colour or it has a rank, acrid or simply bad smell, do not buy or eat it under any circumstances.

Take special care when preparing raw meat and fish. A separate chopping board should be used for each, and the knife, board and your hands should be thoroughly washed before handling or preparing any other food.

Regularly clean, defrost and clear out the refrigerator or freezer – it is worth checking the packaging to see exactly how long each product is safe to freeze. Avoid handling food if suffering from an upset stomach as bacteria can be passed on through food preparation.

Dish cloths and tea towels must be washed and changed regularly. Ideally use disposable cloths which should be replaced on a daily basis. More durable cloths should be left to soak in bleach, then washed in the washing machine at a high temperature.

Keep your hands, cooking utensils and food preparation surfaces clean and do not allow pets to climb on to any work surfaces.

Buying

Avoid bulk buying where possible, especially fresh produce such as meat, poultry, fish, fruit and vegetables. Fresh foods lose their nutritional value rapidly, so buying a little at a time minimises loss of nutrients. It also means your fridge will not be so full, which reduces the effectiveness of the refrigeration process.

When buying prepackaged goods such as cans or pots of cream and yogurts, check that the packaging is intact and not damaged or pierced at all. Cans should not be dented, pierced or rusty. Check the sell-by dates even for cans and packets of dry ingredients such as flour and rice. Store fresh foods in the refrigerator as soon as possible – not in the car or the office.

When buying frozen foods, ensure that they are not heavily iced on the outside and that the contents feel completely frozen. Ensure that the frozen foods have been stored in the cabinet at the correct storage level and the temperature is below -18°C/-0.4°F. Pack in cool bags to transport home and place in the freezer as soon as possible after purchase.

Preparation

Make sure that all work surfaces and utensils are clean and dry. Hygiene should be given priority at all times. Separate chopping boards should be used for raw and cooked meats, fish and vegetables. Currently, a variety of good quality plastic boards come in various designs and colours. This makes differentiating easier and the plastic has the added hygienic advantage of being washable at high temperatures in the dishwasher. If using the board for fish, first wash in cold water, then in hot to prevent odour. Also remember that knives and utensils should always be thoroughly cleaned after use.

When cooking, be particularly careful to keep cooked and raw food separate to avoid any contamination. It is worth washing all fruits and vegetables regardless of whether they are going to be eaten raw or lightly cooked. This rule should apply even to prewashed herbs and salads.

Do not reheat food more than once. If using a microwave, always check that the food is piping hot all the way through – in theory, the food should reach 70°C/158°F and needs to be cooked at that temperature for at least three minutes to ensure that all bacteria are killed.

All poultry must be thoroughly thawed before using, including chicken and poussin. Remove the food to be thawed from the freezer and place in a shallow dish to contain the juices. Leave the food in the refrigerator until it is completely thawed. A 1.4 kg/3 lb whole chicken will take about 26–30 hours to thaw. To speed up the process, immerse the chicken in cold water, making sure that the water is changed regularly. When the joints can move freely and no ice crystals remain in the cavity, the bird is completely thawed.

Once thawed, remove the wrapper and pat the chicken dry. Place the chicken in a shallow dish, cover lightly and store as close to the base of the refrigerator as possible. The chicken should be cooked as soon as possible.

Some foods can be cooked from

frozen including many prepacked foods such as soups, sauces, casseroles and breads. Where applicable follow the manufacturers' instructions.

Vegetables and fruits can also be cooked from frozen, but meats and fish should be thawed first. The only time food can be refrozen is when the food has been thoroughly thawed then cooked. Once the food has cooled then it can be frozen again, but it should only be stored for one month.

All poultry and game (except for duck) must be cooked thoroughly. When cooked, the juices will run clear on the thickest part of the bird – the best area to try is usually the thigh. Other meats, like minced meat and pork should be cooked right the way through. Fish should turn opaque, be firm in texture and break easily into large flakes.

When cooking leftovers, make sure they are reheated until piping hot and that any sauce or soup reaches boiling point first.

Storing, Refrigerating and Freezing

Meat, poultry, fish, seafood and dairy products should all be refrigerated. The temperature of the refrigerator should be between 1–5°C/34–41°F while the freezer temperature should not rise above -18°C/-0.4°F.

To ensure the optimum refrigerator and freezer temperature, avoid leaving the door open for long periods of time. Try not to overstock the refrigerator as this reduces the airflow inside and therefore the effectiveness in cooling the food within.

When refrigerating cooked food, allow it to cool down quickly and completely before refrigerating. Hot food will raise the temperature of the refrigerator and possibly affect or spoil other food stored in it.

Food within the refrigerator and freezer should always be covered. Raw and cooked food should be stored in separate parts of the refrigerator. Cooked food should be kept on the top shelves of the refrigerator, while raw meat, poultry and fish should be placed on bottom shelves to avoid

drips and cross-contamination. It is recommended that eggs should be refrigerated in order to maintain their freshness and shelf life.

Take care that frozen foods are not stored in the freezer for too long. Blanched vegetables can be stored for one month; beef, lamb, poultry and pork for six months and unblanched vegetables and fruits in syrup for a year. Oily fish and sausages should be stored for three months. Dairy products can last four to six months, while cakes and pastries can be kept in the freezer for three to six months.

High Risk Foods

Certain foods may carry risks to people who are considered vulnerable such as the elderly, the ill, pregnant women, babies, young infants and those suffering from a recurring illness.

It is advisable to avoid those foods listed below which belong to a higher-risk category.

There is a slight chance that some eggs carry the bacteria salmonella. Cook the eggs until both the yolk and the white are firm to eliminate this risk. Pay particular attention to dishes and products incorporating lightly cooked or raw eggs which should be eliminated from the diet. Hollandaise sauce, mayonnaise, mousses, soufflés and meringues all use raw or lightly cooked eggs, as do custard-based dishes, ice creams and sorbets. These are all considered high-risk foods to the vulnerable groups mentioned above.

Certain meats and poultry also carry the potential risk of salmonella and so should be cooked thoroughly

until the juices run clear and there is no pinkness left. Unpasteurised products such as milk, cheese (especially soft cheese), pâté, meat (both raw and cooked) all have the potential risk of listeria and should be avoided.

When buying seafood, buy from a reputable source which has a high turnover to ensure freshness. Fish should have bright clear eyes, shiny skin and bright pink or red gills. The fish should feel stiff to the touch, with a slight smell of sea air and iodine. The flesh of fish steaks and fillets should be translucent with no signs of discolouration. Molluscs such as scallops, clams and mussels are sold fresh and are still alive. Avoid any that are open or do not close when tapped lightly. In the same way, univalves such as cockles or winkles should withdraw back into their shells when lightly prodded. When choosing cephalopods such as squid and octopus they should have a firm flesh and pleasant sea smell.

As with all fish, whether it is shellfish or seafish, care is required when freezing it. It is imperative to check whether the fish has been frozen before. If it has been frozen, then it should not be frozen again under any circumstances.

Pasta Techniques and Tips

Steps to Cooking Perfect Pasta

Follow a few simple rules to ensure that your pasta is cooked to perfection every time:

1 Choose a big saucepan – there needs to be plenty of room for the pasta to move around during cooking so that it does not stick together. The most convenient type of saucepan has a built-in perforated inner pan, so that the pasta can be lifted out of the water and drained as soon as it is cooked.

2 Cook the pasta in a large quantity of fast-boiling, well-salted water; ideally about 4 litres/7 pints of water and 1½–2 tablespoons of salt for every 350 g/12 oz–450 g/1 lb of pasta. Some cooks say that the addition of 1–2 teaspoons of olive or sunflower oil not only helps to stop the water boiling over but also helps to prevent the pasta from sticking. However, other cooks believe that as long as the saucepan is large enough and the water is on a full-rolling boil, the pasta will not stick together nor will the water boil over.

3 Tip in the pasta all at once, give it a stir and cover with a lid. Quickly bring back to a rolling boil then remove the lid – do not cover with a lid during cooking. Once it is boiling, turn down the heat to medium-high and cook the pasta for the required time. It should be 'al dente' which literally translates as 'to the tooth' and means that the pasta should be tender, but still firm to the bite. Test frequently towards the end of cooking time; the only way to do this is to take out a piece and try it. Stir the pasta occasionally during cooking with a wooden spoon or fork to make sure that it does not stick to the pan.

4 As soon as the pasta is ready, drain in a colander (or by lifting the draining

pan up and out of the water if you have a pasta pot with an inner drainer). Give it a shake, so that any trapped water can drain out. At this stage you can toss the pasta in a little oil or butter if you are not mixing it with a sauce. Reserve a little of the cooking water to stir into the pasta, this not only helps to thin the sauce if necessary, but also helps prevent the cooked pasta sticking together as it cools.

Some pastas need a little more care when cooking than others. Never stir stuffed pastas vigorously, or they may split open and the filling will be lost in the cooking water. When cooking long, dried pasta such as spaghetti, you will need to coil the pasta into the water as it starts to soften. Hold one end of the strands of spaghetti and push the other to the bottom of the pan, coiling them round, and using a wooden spoon or fork, when the boiling water gets too close to your hand.

An alternative cooking method is to add the pasta to boiling salted water as before, then boil rapidly for 2 minutes. Cover the pan with a tight-fitting lid and turn off the heat. Leave to stand for the full cooking time, then drain and serve in the usual way. Pasta may also be cooked successfully in a microwave, although it does not cook any faster than on the hob. Put the pasta in a large bowl, add salt, then pour over enough boiling water to cover the pasta by at least 2.5 cm/1 inch. Microwave on high (100% power) for the times given below. Allow the pasta to stand for 2–3 minutes before draining.

Pasta Cooking Times

Start timing from the moment that the pasta returns to the boil; not from when it was added. Use a kitchen timer if possible, as even a few seconds too long may spoil the pasta.

Fresh 2–3 minutes for thin noodles (although very fine pastas may be ready within seconds of the pasta

boiling), thick noodles and shapes 3–4 minutes and filled pastas 5–7 minutes.

Dried 8–12 minutes; filled pastas can take up to 20 minutes to cook, however, you should always check the instructions, as some pastas labelled 'quick cook' only take about 4 minutes.

Serving Quantities

As an approximate guide, allow 75–125 g (3–4 oz) uncooked pasta per person. Obviously the amount will depend on whether the pasta is being served for a light or main meal and the type of sauce that it is being served with.

Matching Pasta Types and Sauces

It is entirely up to you which pasta you serve with which sauce but in general, heavier sauces with large chunks of meat or vegetables go less with pastas that will trap the sauce and meat in curls and hollows, such as penne, shells, riagatoni or spirals. On the other hand, soft fluid sauces suit long pastas such as linguine, pappardelle, or tagliatelle.

Classic Sauces
Alla Carbonara Pasta with ham, eggs and cream – the heat of the pasta cooks the eggs to thicken the sauce.

Alla Napoletana Made from fresh tomatoes, but with olive oil, garlic and onions.

All'arrabiata A hot sauce with red chillies, tomatoes and chopped bacon.

All'aglio e Olio Pasta with olive oil and finely chopped garlic.

Alla Marinara A fresh tomato and basil sauce, sometimes with wine (not seafood).

Con Ragu Meat sauce from Bologna (known as bolognese sauce in English), often made with half minced pork and half minced beef. This is traditionally served with tagliatelle and not spaghetti.

Serving Pasta

In Italy, pasta is usually dressed with the sauce before serving to combine the flavours, but you can top the pasta with the sauce if you prefer, in which case, toss it in a little olive oil or butter to give it an attractive sheen. Cook the sauce and pasta so that they will both be ready at the same time; most sauces can be left to stand for a few minutes and reheated when the pasta is ready. If the pasta is ready before the sauce, drain it, and return to the pan with a tight-fitting lid – it should be fine for a few minutes. Always serve in warmed serving bowls or plates, as pasta loses heat very quickly.

Serving Wines with Pasta

If possible, choose a wine that comes from the same region as the dish you are serving. If there is wine in the sauce, you will be able to serve the rest of the bottle with your meal, so make sure you choose one that you enjoy drinking. Otherwise, pick a wine that matches the strongest-flavoured ingredient in the sauce. Rich, meaty sauces or highly spiced ones with lots of garlic need a robust, full-bodied wine to go with them. Of course, there is no reason why you should stick to Italian wines and if you are serving an oriental pasta dish you may opt for lager or other drinks. Below are ten well-known types of Italian wine.

White Wines
Chardonnay This wine is produced in many parts of the world and is wonderful served with fish dishes. The Italian chardonnay has a faint lemony flavour.

Frascati This wine is made near Rome and is one of the most popular Italian wines. It is crisp and fruity and has quite a lot of body. It goes well with most foods.

Orvieto This wine is named after the town of the same name, just north of Rome. It is dry and soft with a slightly nutty and fruity flavour and is good for summer drinking and serving with fish and white meats.

Soave This wine is one of Italy's most famous wines. The best ones have a distinct hint of almonds and are dry and crisp. It goes well with shellfish, chicken and light vegetable pasta sauces.

Verdiccho This wine comes in a carved amphora bottle and in Italy is known as La Lollobrigida. A crisp, clean and dry white wine with a slightly metallic edge, it is best when served with fish and seafood.

Red Wines
Barbaresco This wine is full-bodied with an intense flavour and a high tannin content. It teams well with rich pasta dishes, especially beef.

Bardolino This is light and fruity with an almost cherry and slightly bitter almond taste; perfect for duck and game.

Barolo This is one of Italy's finest wines and is a full-bodied red. Serve with rich meaty dishes, game or spicy sausage pasta sauces.

Chianti This wine is best drunk when young and may be served slightly chilled. It is often regarded as the classic accompaniment to pasta.

Pasta Equipment

When making and cooking pasta, a bare minimum of equipment is needed; some would say that a rolling pin, a large pan and a colander would suffice, however, there are many gadgets that make the process a lot easier.

When Making
Rolling pin
Try to use one that is quite slender and choose a conventional wooden one without handles. In Italy pasta rolling pins are very long, for rolling out large quantities of pasta at a time, and slightly thicker in the middle with tapering ends.

Pasta machine A traditional, hand-cranked pasta machine has adjusting rollers and usually cutters for making tagliatelle and finer tagliarini. More complicated ones come with a selection of cutters.

Pasta wheel This is useful for cutting noodles such as tagliatelle and pappardelle if you do not have a pasta machine and also for stuffed shapes such as ravioli. This is an inexpensive piece of equipment and less likely to drag or tear the pasta than a knife.

Ravioli cutter Specially designed, fluted-edged cutters can be bought for cutting pasta. A fluted or plain biscuit cutter works just as well.

When Cooking and Serving
Long-handled pasta fork This is useful for stirring the pasta to keep the pieces separate during cooking. You can also get wooden pasta hooks which will lift out the strands of pasta so that you can check whether or not it is cooked.

Parmesan graters These range from simple hand graters to electrical gadgets. If sharp, the fine side of a box grater works equally well.

Parmesan knife This is used to shave Parmesan off a block. A vegetable peeler may be used as an alternative.

Pasta cooking pot Officially this should be tall with straight sides and handles and should have an inner basket. When buying, choose one that is not too heavy, and will be easy to manage when full.

Pasta measurer This is a wooden gadget with several holes for measuring spaghetti. Each hole takes a different amount of pasta for a given number of people.

Fresh Ingredients

Thai and Chinese cooking is amongst the world's greatest. In both, the basic philosophy of balance is the same, where the freshest produce is combined with the flavours of dried, salted and fermented ingredients, preserves and condiments. Most ingredients are now available in ordinary supermarkets and a few of the more unusual ones in Asian or Chinese groceries and markets.

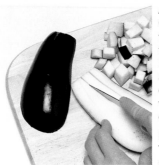

AUBERGINES
Chinese aubergines are thinner with a more delicate flavour than the Mediterranean variety. They are used in many savoury dishes and in Thailand, some varieties are eaten raw with a dip or sauce.

BABY SWEETCORN
These tiny, tender cobs of sweetcorn, about 7.5 cm/ 3 inches long, add a crunchy texture and sweet flavour to many dishes. When buying, make sure that they are bright yellow with no brown patches, firm and crisp.

BAMBOO SHOOTS
Bamboo shoots are young, creamy-coloured, conical-shaped shoots of edible bamboo plants. They add a crunchy texture and clean, mild flavour to many dishes and are sometimes available in Chinese groceries, as well as vacuum-packed or canned in most supermarkets. If you buy the latter, transfer them to a container of water once the can has been opened. If you change the water daily, they will keep for up to five days in the refrigerator.

BASIL
Holy basil with small, dark leaves and purple stalks is frequently used in Thai cooking, although sweet basil, more easily obtainable here, may be used instead.

BEANSPROUTS
These are the shoots of the mung bean and are readily available prepacked in the vegetable section of most supermarkets. They add a wonderfully crisp texture when added to stir-fries and take only a minute or two to cook. Ideally, the brown root should be removed from each sprout and discarded, however, this is time consuming, but improves the appearance of the dish.

BLACK BEANS
These small, black soya beans may also be known as salted black beans, as they have been fermented with salt and spices. Sold loose in Chinese groceries, but also available canned, they have a rich flavour and are often used with ginger and garlic with which they have a particular affinity.

BOK CHOI
Also known as pak choi, the most common variety has long, slightly ridged white stems like celery and large, oval thick dark green leaves. Bok choi has a mild, fresh, slightly peppery taste and needs very little cooking. Choose smaller ones if possible, as they are more tender. Store in the bottom of the refrigerator.

CHILLIES
There are many different kinds of chillies and generally, the smaller they are the more fierce the heat. Red chillies are generally milder than green ones because they sweeten as they become riper. The tiny, slender tapering red or green Thai chillies are very hot and pungent. Thai cooks often include the seeds in cooking, but to moderate the heat, scrape out and discard the seeds.

CHINESE CELERY
Unlike the Western variety, Chinese celery stalks are thin, hollow and very crisp and range from pure white to dark green. Used as both a herb and a vegetable, Chinese celery is often stir-fried or used in soups and braised dishes.

CHINESE KALE
This green vegetable is popular in Thai cuisine. It has an almost earthy and slightly bitter taste and is usually served blanched and accompanied by oyster sauce. When buying, look for firm stems and fresh, dark green leaves. Store in the bottom drawer of the refrigerator for up to four days.

CHINESE KEYS
Despite its name, this root vegetable is often used in Thai cuisine and rarely in Chinese. It is a member of the ginger family, with an aromatic sweet flavour that goes well in Thai curries.

CHINESE LEAVES
Also known as Chinese cabbage, Chinese leaves look like a large, tightly packed lettuce with crinkly, pale green leaves. It adds a crunchy texture to stir-fries.

CHINESE MUSTARD CABBAGE
Also known as gaai choi, these mustard plants are similar in appearance to cabbages. The whole leaf is eaten, usually shredded into soups and stir-fries to which they add a fresh astringent flavour.

CORIANDER
Fresh coriander is the most popular fresh herb used in Thai cooking. It has an appearance similar to flat-leaf parsley, but has a pungent, slightly citrus flavour. Leaves, stems and roots are all used, so buy in big fresh bunches if possible.

DURIAN
This large, spiky-skinned tropical fruit has such an unpleasantly strong aroma that it is banned from public transport and hotels in Bangkok. It is expensive to buy a whole fruit, but you can sometimes buy frozen packs of skinless pieces of fruit.

GALANGAL
This is a rhizome, called laos or ka in Thailand. It is similar to ginger, but the skin is a pinkish colour and the flavour more complex and mellow. Peel it thinly and slice or grate the flesh. When sliced, it can be kept in an airtight container in the refrigerator for up to two weeks. If unavailable, ginger is an acceptable substitute.

GARLIC

This popular seasoning flavours almost all Thai and many Chinese dishes. In Thailand, garlic heads are smaller and thinner skinned, so they are often used whole as well as finely chopped or crushed. Choose firm garlic, preferably with a pinkish tinge and store in a cool, dry place, but not in the refrigerator.

GINGER

Fresh root ginger has a pungent, spicy, fresh taste. It is usually peeled, then finely chopped or grated – vary the amount of ginger used to suit your own taste. For just a hint, slice thickly and add to the dish when cooking, then remove just before serving. Fresh ginger is infinitely preferable to the powdered variety, which loses its flavour rapidly. Fresh ginger should feel firm when you buy it. If you have more than you need it can be used within a week. Store it in the freezer as it can be grated from frozen.

KAFFIR LIME LEAVES

Dark green, smooth, glossy leaves, these come from the kaffir lime tree and are highly sought after for Thai cooking. They add a distinctive citrus flavour to curries, soups and sauces. Buy them from larger supermarkets and Oriental grocery shops and keep them in a sealed polythene bag in the freezer. Lime zest can be used as an alternative.

KRACHAI

Also known as lesser ginger, this is smaller and more spicy than either ginger or galangal. It can be bought fresh in Oriental food shops or dried in small packets.

LEMON GRASS

These look a bit like spring onions, but are much tougher. The stems should be bashed to release the lemony flavour during cooking, then removed before serving. Alternatively, peel away the outer layers and chop the heart very finely.

LOTUS ROOT

This is the underwater rhizome of the lotus flower and has a lacy appearance when sliced and a sweet, crunchy flavour. Fresh lotus root takes about two hours to cook, so it is worth considering using canned lotus root instead.

MANGETOUT

These tender green pea pods with flat, barely formed peas have a deliciously crisp texture. To prepare them for cooking, simply top and tail, pulling away any string from the edges.

MOOLI

Also known as daikon or white radish, these look like smooth, white parsnips (they come from the same family as the radish). They have a peppery, fresh taste and are often used in salads, peeled and thinly sliced or grated. They can also be cooked, but because they have a high water content, they should be salted to extract some of the liquid, then rinsed well and steamed or boiled. They are often carved into beautiful and intricate shapes as a table decoration or garnish.

MUSHROOMS

Oyster mushrooms with their subtle flavour and delicate, almost slippery texture often feature in Chinese cooking. Now cultivated, they are widely available. The colour of the fan-shaped cap gives the mushroom its name, although they can also be pink or yellow as well as grey. Tear into long triangular segments, following the lines of the gills, and cook the smaller ones whole. Shiitake mushrooms were originally Oriental, but they are now grown all over the world. They are more often used dried in Chinese cooking, but may also be used fresh – the caps have a strong flavour and are generally sliced and the stalks discarded. Cook the mushrooms gently for a short time, as they may toughen if overcooked. Straw mushrooms are sometimes known as double mushrooms because that is exactly what they look like; two mushrooms that grow end to end. They are small and pale brown with a pale-coloured stem.

PAPAYA

Also called pawpaw, the unripe green flesh of this tropical fruit is often used in Thai cooking. It ripens to a deep orange colour and is delicious sliced and served as a dessert.

SHALLOTS

Small, mild-flavoured members of the onion family, shallots have coppery-coloured skins. Use them in the same way as onions, or thinly slice and deep-fry to use as a garnish.

SPRING ONIONS

Long, slender spring onions are the immature bulbs of yellow onions. They are frequently used in stir fries, as they cook within minutes.

TAMARIND

This adds an essential sour taste to many dishes. It is extracted from the pods as a sticky brown pulp, which is soaked to make tamarind water.

TOFU

Tofu or bean curd has been used as an ingredient in Thai and Chinese cooking for over 1000 years. Made from yellow soya beans, which are soaked, ground and briefly cooked, tofu is very rich in protein and low in calories. Because of its bland taste it is ideal cooked with stronger flavourings. It is usually available in two types: a soft variety known as silken tofu that can be used for soups and desserts, and a firm, solid white block, which can be cubed or sliced and included in stir-frying and braising. Also available is smoked tofu, which is a seasoned bean curd. When using, cut into the required size with care and do not stir too much when cooking; it simply needs to be heated through.

WATER CHESTNUTS

These are bulbs of an Asian water plant that look like and are a similar size to chestnuts. When peeled, the inner flesh is very crisp. Some Oriental grocers sell them fresh, although canned, either whole or sliced, are almost as good.

WATER SPINACH

This is widely grown throughout Asia and is unrelated to ordinary spinach. The leaves are elongated and tender and the stems fine and delicate. Water spinach requires minimal cooking. It is cooked in the same way as spinach, either steamed, stir-fried or added to soups.

YARD-LONG BEANS

Although unrelated to French beans, they are similar in appearance, but about four times longer. As they grow, they start to curl and are often sold in looped bunches. Two varieties exist: a pale green type and a much darker, thinner variety. They are very popular and may be found in great quantities in Chinese markets. The Cantonese often cook them with black beans or fermented bean curd and in Sichuan, they are deep-fried. Store in a plastic bag in the refrigerator for up to four days. To prepare, cut into lengths and use in exactly the same way as French beans.

Cooking Techniques for Rice

There are countless ways to cook rice and there are even more opinions about how to do so! Much, of course, depends on the variety and brand of rice being used, the dish being prepared and the desired results. Each variety of rice has its own characteristics. Some types of rice cook to light, separate grains; some to a rich, creamy consistency; and some to a consistency where the grains stick together. It is important, therefore, to ensure that the appropriate rice is used. Different types of rice have very different powers of absorption. Long-grain rice will absorb about three times its weight in water, whereas just 25 g/1 oz of plump and short-grained pudding rice can soak up a massive 300 ml/½ pint of liquid.

Cooking Long-grain Rice

By far the simplest method of cooking long-grain rice – whether white, brown or basmati – is to add it to plenty of boiling, salted water in a large saucepan, so that the rice grains can move freely and do not stick together. Allow about 50 g/2 oz of rice per person when cooking as an accompaniment. Rinse it under cold, running water until clear – this removes any starch still clinging to the grains – then tip into the rapidly boiling water. Stir once, then when the water comes back to the boil, turn down the heat a little and simmer uncovered, allowing 10–12 minutes for white rice and 30–40 minutes for brown (check the packet timings, as brands of rice vary). The easiest way to test if the rice is cooked is to bite a couple of grains – they should be tender but still firm. Drain the rice straight away, then return to the pan with a little butter and herbs if liked. Fluff the grains with a fork and serve. If you need to keep the rice warm, put it in a bowl and place over a pan of barely simmering water. Cover the top of the bowl with a clean tea towel until ready to serve.

Absorption Method

Cooking rice using the absorption method is also very simple and is favoured by many because no draining is involved and therefore no water is wasted. Also, by using this method, stock and other flavourful ingredients can be added and will be absorbed by the rice. Furthermore, valuable nutrients are retained that would otherwise be lost in the cooking water when drained. To cook rice this way, weigh out the quantity of rice you require, then measure it by volume in a measuring jug – you will need about 150 ml/¼ pint for two people. Briefly rinse the rice in a sieve under cold running water, then tip into a large heavy based saucepan. If liked, you can cook the rice in a little butter or oil for about 1 minute. Pour in two parts water to one part rice (or use stock if you prefer), season with salt and bring to the boil uncovered. Cover the pan with a tight-fitting lid, then simmer gently without lifting the lid, until the liquid is absorbed and the rice is tender. White rice will take 15 minutes to cook, whereas brown rice will take about 35 minutes. It is important to simmer over a very low heat or the liquid will cook away before the rice is ready. Do not be tempted to check the rice too often while it is cooking as you will let out steam and therefore moisture. If there is still a little liquid left when the rice is tender, remove the lid and cook for about a minute until evaporated. Remove from the heat and leave to stand with the lid on for 4–5 minutes. Do not rinse the rice when it is cooked, just fluff up with a fork before serving. This method is also good for cooking Jasmine and Valencia rice.

Oven-baked Method

The oven-baked method also works by absorption. It takes a little longer than cooking rice on the hob, but is ideal to add to the oven if you are roasting or simmering a casserole.

To make oven-baked rice for two people, gently fry a chopped onion in 1 tablespoon of olive oil in a 1.1 litre/2 pint flameproof casserole dish until soft and golden (leave the onion out if preferred). Add 75 g/3 oz long-grain rice and cook for 1 minute, then stir in 300 ml/½ pint of stock – you can also add a finely pared strip of lemon rind or a bay leaf at this stage. Cover with a lid or tinfoil and bake on the middle shelf of a preheated oven at 180°C/350°F/Gas Mark 4 for 40 minutes, or until the rice is tender and all the stock has been absorbed. Fluff up with a fork before serving.

Cooking in the Microwave

Rinse long-grain white or brown rice in cold running water, then place in a large heat-proof bowl. Add boiling water or stock to the bowl, allowing 300 ml/ $^1/_2$ pint for 125 g/4 oz rice and 550 ml/ 18 fl oz for 225 g/8 oz rice. Add a pinch of salt and a knob of butter, if desired. Cover with clingfilm, making a few air holes to allow the steam to escape and microwave on high for 3 minutes. Stir, then re-cover and microwave on medium for 12 minutes for white rice and 25 minutes for brown. Leave to stand, covered, for 5 minutes before fluffing up with a fork and serving.

In a Pressure Cooker

Follow the quantities given for the absorption method and bring to the boil in the pressure cooker. Stir once, cover with the lid and bring to a high 6.8 kg/15 lb pressure. Lower the heat and cook for 5 minutes if white rice or cook for 8 minutes if brown rice.

In a Rice Cooker

Follow the quantities given for the absorption method. Put the rice, salt and boiling water or stock in the cooker, bring back to the boil and cover. When all the liquid has been absorbed the cooker will turn itself off automatically.

Wild Rice

This type of rice can be cooked by any of the methods used for long-grain rice, but the cooking time required is longer. It will take between 35–50 minutes to cook wild rice, depending on whether you like your rice slightly chewy or very tender. To speed up the cooking time by 5–10 minutes, soak the rice in cold water first for 30 minutes. This also increases the volume of the rice when it is cooked.

Red Rice

Cook this in the same way as brown rice as this type of rice has a very hard grain. It is best to cook the rice for about 40–60 minutes if you like your rice really tender – it will still keep its shape.

Risotto Rice

Most rices should not be stirred during cooking as it breaks up the grains and makes them soggy. Risotto rice is different as it can absorb nearly five times its weight in liquid and still retains its shape. A good risotto has a creamy texture, with a slight bite to the individual grains and is made by adding the cooking liquid gradually and stirring almost continuously during cooking.

For a classic risotto (known as *alla Milanese*) for four people, place 1 tablespoon of olive oil and a knob of butter in a large heavy based saucepan. Slowly heat the butter and oil until the butter has melted. Add 1 chopped onion to the pan and cook until tender. Add 150 ml/$^1/_4$ pint of dry white wine and boil rapidly until almost totally reduced. Stir in 300 g/11 oz risotto rice. Add 1 litre/1$^3/_4$ pints boiling vegetable or chicken stock, a ladleful at a time – each ladleful should be completely absorbed by the rice before the next one is added. Continue adding the stock until the rice is tender. This will take 15–20 minutes, although it may not be necessary to add all of the stock to achieve the desired consistency. Serve the risotto straight away, sprinkled with grated Parmesan cheese. The basic risotto can be flavoured in many ways. Try adding a couple of bay leaves, a lemon grass stalk or a large pinch of saffron to the stock, or use more red or white wine and less stock.

Glutinous Rice

This rice is steamed (instead of being cooked in boiling water) until the grains are soft, tender and stick together in a mass. Cooking times vary slightly according to the brand, so check the packet instructions for specific directions.

Pudding Rice

For a simple rice pudding put 50 g/ 2 oz of pudding rice in a buttered 1.2 litre/2 pint ovenproof dish with sugar to taste. Pour over 600 ml/1 pint of near-boiling milk and bake in a preheated oven at 150°C/300°F/Gas Mark 2 for 30 minutes. Stir, then bake for a further 1–1$^1/_4$ hours until tender. Vary the flavour by infusing the milk with orange rind, adding nuts and dried fruit to the mixture or using 300 ml/$^1/_2$ pint coconut milk or single cream and 300 ml/$^1/_2$ pint of milk instead of milk alone.

Health and Nutrition

Rice has been the dietary staple of the East for centuries where it has provided a healthy, balanced diet and has added substance to the small quantities of meat used in Eastern cooking. It is low in fat and high in complex carbohydrates which are absorbed slowly, helping to maintain blood sugar levels. Rice is also a reasonable source of protein and provides most of the B vitamins and the minerals potassium and phosphorus. It is also a gluten-free cereal, making it suitable for coeliacs. Like other unrefined grains, brown rice is richer in nutrients and fibre than refined white rice.

Herbs and Spices

Herbs are easy to grow and a garden is not needed as they can easily thrive on a small patio, window box or even on a windowsill. It is worth the effort to plant a few herbs as they do not require much attention or nurturing. The reward will be a range of fresh herbs available whenever needed, and fresh flavours that cannot be beaten to add to any dish that is being prepared. While fresh herbs should be picked or bought as close as possible to the time of use, freeze-dried and dried herbs and spices will usually keep for around six months. The best idea is to buy little and often, and to store the herbs in airtight jars in a cool dark cupboard. Fresh herbs tend to have a milder flavour than dried and equate to around one level tablespoon of fresh to one level teaspoon of dried. As a result, quantities used in cooking should be altered accordingly. A variety of herbs and spices and their uses are listed below.

ALLSPICE
The dark allspice berries come whole or ground and have a flavour similar to that of cinnamon, cloves and nutmeg. Although not the same as mixed spices, allspice can be used with pickles, relishes, cakes and milk puddings or whole in meat and fish dishes.

ANISEED
Aniseed comes in whole seeds or ground. It has a strong aroma and flavour and should be used sparingly in baking and salad dressings.

BASIL
Best fresh but also available in dried form, basil can be used raw or cooked. It works well in many dishes but is particularly well suited to tomato-based dishes and sauces, salads and Mediterranean recipes.

BAY LEAVES
Bay leaves are available in fresh or dried form as well as ground. They make up part of a bouquet garni and are particularly delicious when added to meat and poultry dishes, soups, stews, vegetable dishes and stuffing. They also impart a spicy flavour to milk puddings and egg custards.

BOUQUET GARNI
Bouquet garni is a bouquet of fresh herbs tied with a piece of string or in a small piece of muslin. It is used to flavour casseroles, stews and stocks or sauces. The herbs that are normally used are parsley, thyme, and bay leaves.

CARAWAY SEEDS
Caraway seeds have a warm sweet taste and are often used in breads and cakes but are delicious with cabbage dishes and pickles as well.

CAYENNE
Cayenne is the powdered form of a red chilli pepper said to be native to Cayenne. It is similar in appearance to paprika and can be used sparingly to add a fiery kick to many dishes.

CARDAMOM
Cardamom has a distinctive sweet, rich taste and can be bought whole in the pod, in seed form or ground. This sweet aromatic spice is delicious in curries, rice, cakes and biscuits and is great served with rice pudding and fruit.

CHERVIL
Reminiscent of parsley and available either in fresh or dried form, chervil has a faintly sweet, spicy flavour and is particularly good in soups, cheese dishes, stews and with eggs.

CHILLI
Available whole, fresh, dried and in powdered form, red chillies tend to be sweeter in taste than their green counterparts. They are particularly associated with Spanish and Mexican-style cooking and curries, but are also delicious with pickles, dips, sauces and in pizza toppings.

CHIVES
Best used when fresh but also available in dried form, this member of the onion family is ideal for use when a delicate onion flavour is required. Chives are good with eggs, cheese, fish and vegetable dishes. They also work well as a garnish for soups, meat and vegetable dishes.

CINNAMON
Cinnamon comes in the form of reddish-brown sticks of bark from an evergreen tree and has a sweet, pungent aroma. Either whole or ground, cinnamon is delicious in cakes and milk puddings, particularly with apple, and is used in mulled wine and for preserving.

CLOVES
Mainly used whole although also available ground, cloves have a very warm, sweet pungent aroma and can be used to stud roast ham and pork, in mulled wine and punch and when pickling fruit. When ground, they can be used in making mincemeat and in Christmas puddings and biscuits.

CORIANDER
Coriander seeds have an orangey flavour and are available whole or ground. Coriander is particularly delicious (whether whole or roughly ground) in casseroles, curries and as a pickling spice. The leaves are used to flavour spicy aromatic dishes as well as a garnish.

CUMIN
Also available ground or as whole seeds, cumin has a strong, slightly bitter flavour. It is one of the main ingredients in curry powder and compliments many fish, meat and rice dishes.

DILL
Dill leaves are available fresh or dried and have a mild flavour, while the seeds are slightly bitter. Dill is particularly good with salmon, new potatoes and in sauces. The seeds are good in pickles and vegetable dishes.

FENNEL
Whole seeds or ground, fennel has a fragrant, sweet aniseed flavour and is sometimes known as the fish herb because it compliments fish dishes so well.

GINGER
Ginger comes in many forms but primarily as a fresh root and in dried ground form, which can be used in baking, curries, pickles, sauces and Chinese cooking.

LEMON GRASS
Available fresh and dried, with a subtle, aromatic, lemony flavour, lemon grass is essential to Thai cooking. It is also delicious when added to soups, poultry and fish dishes.

MACE
The outer husk of nutmeg has a milder nutmeg flavour and can be used in pickles, cheese dishes, stewed fruits, sauces and hot punch.

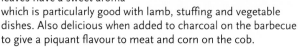

MARJORAM
Often dried, marjoram has a sweet slightly spicy flavour, which tastes fantastic when added to stuffing, meat or tomato-based dishes.

MINT
Available fresh or dried, mint has a strong, sweet aroma which is delicious in a sauce or jelly to serve with lamb. It is also great with fresh peas and new potatoes and is an essential ingredient in Pimms.

MUSTARD SEED
These yellow and brown seeds are available whole or ground and are often found in pickles, relishes, cheese dishes, dressings, curries and as an accompaniment to meat.

NUTMEG
The large whole seeds have a warm, sweet taste and compliment custards, milk puddings, cheese dishes, parsnips and creamy soups.

OREGANO
The strongly flavoured dried leaves of oregano are similar to marjoram and are used extensively in Italian and Greek cooking.

PAPRIKA
Paprika often comes in two varieties. One is quite sweet and mild and the other has a slight bite to it. Paprika is made from the fruit of the sweet pepper and is good in meat and poultry dishes as well as a garnish. The rule of buying herbs and spices little and often applies particularly to paprika as unfortunately it does not keep particularly well.

PARSLEY
The stems as well as the leaves of parsley can be used to compliment most savoury dishes as they contain the most flavour. They can also be used as a garnish.

PEPPER
This comes in white and black peppercorns and is best freshly ground. Both add flavour to most dishes, sauces and gravies. Black pepper has a more robust flavour, while white pepper is much more delicate.

POPPY SEEDS
These tiny, grey-black coloured seeds impart a sweet, nutty flavour when added to biscuits, vegetable dishes, dressings and cheese dishes.

ROSEMARY
Delicious fresh or dried, these small, needle-like leaves have a sweet aroma which is particularly good with lamb, stuffing and vegetable dishes. Also delicious when added to charcoal on the barbecue to give a piquant flavour to meat and corn on the cob.

SAFFRON
Deep orange in colour, saffron is traditionally used in paella, rice and cakes but is also delicious with poultry. Saffron is the most expensive of all spices.

SAGE
Fresh or dried sage leaves have a pungent, slightly bitter taste which is delicious with pork and poultry, sausages, stuffing and with stuffed pasta when tossed in a little butter and fresh sage.

SAVORY
This herb resembles thyme, but has a softer flavour that particularly compliments all types of fish and beans.

SESAME
Sesame seeds have a nutty taste, especially when toasted, and are delicious in baking, on salads, or with Far-Eastern cooking.

TARRAGON
The fresh or dried leaves of tarragon have a sweet aromatic taste which is particularly good with poultry, seafood, fish, creamy sauces and stuffing.

THYME
Available fresh or dried, thyme has a pungent flavour and is included in bouquet garni. It compliments many meat and poultry dishes and stuffing.

TURMERIC
Turmeric is obtained from the root of a lily from southeast Asia. This root is ground and has a brilliant yellow colour. It has a bitter, peppery flavour and is often combined for use in curry powder and mustard. Also delicious in pickles, relishes and dressings.

Soups
& Starters

This section enables you to prepare a dazzling range of mouth-watering starters from across the globe. Whatever their country of origin, you can prepare these appetizing dishes swiftly and easily in your own kitchen by following the step-by-step instructions and helpful picture guides.

Iced Gazpacho

INGREDIENTS

Serves 4–6

2 ripe red peppers
1 cucumber
400 g/14 oz large, juicy tomatoes,
   skinned, deseeded and
   coarsely chopped
4 tbsp olive oil
2 tbsp sherry vinegar
salt and pepper

For the garlic croûtons:

2 tbsp olive oil
1 garlic clove, halved
2 slices bread, crusts removed and
   cut into 5 mm/$\frac{1}{4}$ inch dice
sea salt

To garnish:

diced green pepper
diced red pepper
finely diced deseeded cucumber
chopped spring onions
ice cubes

1 Cut the peppers in half and remove the cores and seeds, then coarsely chop. Peel the cucumber, cut it in half lengthways, then cut into quarters. Remove the seeds with a teaspoon, then coarsely chop the flesh.

2 Put the peppers, cucumber, tomatoes, olive oil and vinegar in a food processor and process until smooth. Season with salt and pepper to taste. Transfer to a bowl, cover and chill for at least 4 hours.

3 Meanwhile, make the garlic croûtons. Heat the oil in a frying pan over a medium-high heat. Add the garlic and fry, stirring, for 2 minutes to flavour the oil.

4 Remove and discard the garlic. Add the diced bread and fry until golden on all sides. Drain well on crumpled paper towels and sprinkle with sea salt. Store in an airtight container if not using at once.

5 To serve, place each of the vegetable garnishes in bowls for guests to add to their soup. Taste the soup and adjust the seasoning if necessary. Put ice cubes into soup bowls and ladle the soup on top. Serve at once.

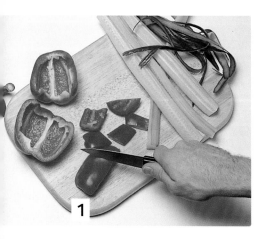

Vietnamese Beef & Rice Noodle Soup

INGREDIENTS

Serves 4–6

For the beef stock:
900 g/2 lb meaty beef bones
1 large onion, peeled and quartered
2 carrots, peeled and cut into chunks
2 celery stalks, trimmed and sliced
1 leek, washed and sliced into chunks
2 garlic cloves, unpeeled and
   lightly crushed
3 whole star anise
1 tsp black peppercorns

For the soup:
175 g/6 oz dried rice stick noodles
4–6 spring onions, trimmed and
   diagonally sliced
1 red chilli, deseeded and
   diagonally sliced
1 small bunch fresh coriander
1 small bunch fresh mint
350 g/12 oz fillet steak, very
   thinly sliced
salt and freshly ground black pepper

1. Place all the ingredients for the beef stock into a large stock pot or saucepan and cover with cold water. Bring to the boil and skim off any scum that rises to the surface. Reduce the heat and simmer gently, partially covered, for 2–3 hours, skimming occasionally.

2. Strain into a large bowl and leave to cool, then skim off the fat. Chill in the refrigerator and, when cold, remove any fat from the surface. Pour 1.7 litres/3 pints of the stock into a large wok and reserve.

3. Cover the noodles with warm water and leave for 3 minutes, or until just softened. Drain, then cut into 10 cm/4 inch lengths.

4. Arrange the spring onions and chilli on a serving platter or large plate. Strip the leaves from the coriander and mint and arrange them in piles on the plate.

5. Bring the stock in the wok to the boil over a high heat. Add the noodles and simmer for about 2 minutes, or until tender. Add the beef strips and simmer for about 1 minute. Season to taste with salt and pepper.

6. Ladle the soup with the noodles and beef strips into individual soup bowls and serve immediately with the plate of condiments handed around separately.

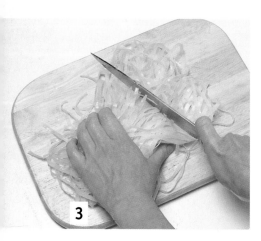

3

4

5

Creamy Caribbean Chicken & Coconut Soup

INGREDIENTS

Serves 4

6–8 spring onions

2 garlic cloves

1 red chilli

175 g/6 oz cooked chicken, shredded
  or diced

2 tbsp vegetable oil

1 tsp ground turmeric

300 ml/½ pint coconut milk

900 ml/1½ pints chicken stock

50 g/2 oz small soup pasta or
  spaghetti, broken into small pieces

½ lemon, sliced

salt and freshly ground black pepper

1–2 tbsp freshly chopped coriander

sprigs of fresh coriander, to garnish

HELPFUL HINT

Be careful handling chillies. Either wear rubber gloves or scrub your hands thoroughly, using plenty of soap and water. Avoid touching eyes or any other sensitive areas.

1 Trim the spring onions and thinly slice; peel the garlic and finely chop. Cut off the top from the chilli, slit down the side and remove seeds and membrane, then finely chop and reserve.

2 Remove and discard any skin or bones from the cooked chicken and shred using 2 forks and reserve.

3 Heat a large wok, add the oil and when hot add the spring onions, garlic and chilli and stir-fry for 2 minutes, or until the onion has softened. Stir in the turmeric and cook for 1 minute.

4 Blend the coconut milk with the chicken stock until smooth, then pour into the wok. Add the pasta or spaghetti with the lemon slices and bring to the boil.

5 Simmer, half-covered, for 10–12 minutes, or until the pasta is tender; stir occasionally.

6 Remove the lemon slices from the wok and add the chicken. Season to taste with salt and pepper and simmer for 2–3 minutes, or until the chicken is heated through thoroughly.

7 Stir in the chopped coriander and ladle into heated bowls. Garnish with sprigs of fresh coriander and serve immediately.

2

3

6

Thai Shellfish Soup

INGREDIENTS

Serves 4–6

350 g/12 oz raw prawns
350 g/12 oz firm white fish, such as
  monkfish, cod or haddock
175 g/ 6 oz small squid rings
1 tbsp lime juice
450 g/1 lb live mussels
400 ml/15 fl oz coconut milk
1 tbsp groundnut oil
2 tbsp Thai red curry paste
1 lemon grass stalk, bruised
3 kaffir lime leaves, finely shredded
2 tbsp Thai fish sauce
salt and freshly ground black pepper
fresh coriander leaves, to garnish

1 Peel the prawns. Using a sharp knife, remove the black vein along the back of the prawns. Pat dry with absorbent kitchen paper and reserve.

2 Skin the fish, pat dry and cut into 2.5 cm/1 inch chunks. Place in a bowl with the prawns and the squid rings. Sprinkle with the lime juice and reserve.

3 Scrub the mussels, removing their beards and any barnacles. Discard any mussels that are open, damaged or that do not close when tapped. Place in a large saucepan and add 150 ml/¼ pint of coconut milk.

4 Cover, bring to the boil, then simmer for 5 minutes, or until the mussels open, shaking the saucepan occasionally. Lift out the mussels, discarding any unopened ones, strain the liquid through a muslin-lined sieve and reserve.

5 Rinse and dry the saucepan. Heat the groundnut oil, add the curry paste and cook for 1 minute, stirring all the time. Add the lemon grass, lime leaves, fish sauce and pour in both the strained and the remaining coconut milk. Bring the contents of the saucepan to a very gentle simmer.

6 Add the fish mixture to the saucepan and simmer for 2–3 minutes or until just cooked. Stir in the mussels, with or without their shells as preferrred. Season to taste with salt and pepper, then garnish with coriander leaves. Ladle into warmed bowls and serve immediately.

FOOD FACT

Sprinkling fish and seafood with lime juice improves its texture, as the acid in the juice firms up the flesh.

2

3

4

White Bean Soup with Parmesan Croûtons

INGREDIENTS

Serves 4

3 thick slices of white bread, cut into
　1 cm/½ inch cubes
3 tbsp groundnut oil
2 tbsp Parmesan cheese, finely grated
1 tbsp light olive oil
1 large onion, peeled and
　finely chopped
50 g/2 oz unsmoked bacon lardons
　(or thick slices of bacon, diced)
1 tbsp fresh thyme leaves
2 x 400 g cannellini beans, drained
900 ml/1½ pints chicken stock
salt and freshly ground black pepper
1 tbsp prepared pesto sauce
50 g/2 oz piece of pepperoni
　sausage, diced
1 tbsp fresh lemon juice
1 tbsp fresh basil, roughly shredded

1　Preheat oven to 200°C/400°F/Gas Mark 6. Place the cubes of bread in a bowl and pour over the groundnut oil. Stir to coat the bread, then sprinkle over the Parmesan cheese. Place on a lightly oiled baking tray and bake in the preheated oven for 10 minutes, or until crisp and golden.

2　Heat the olive oil in a large saucepan and cook the onion for 4–5 minutes until softened. Add the bacon and thyme and cook for a further 3 minutes. Stir in the beans, stock and black pepper and simmer gently for 5 minutes.

3　Place half the bean mixture and liquid into a food processor and blend until smooth.

4　Return the purée to the saucepan. Stir in the pesto sauce, pepperoni sausage and lemon juice and season to taste with salt and pepper.

5　Return the soup to the heat and cook for a further 2–3 minutes, or until piping hot. Place some of the beans in each serving bowl and add a ladleful of soup. Garnish with shredded basil and serve immediately with the croûtons scattered over the top.

1

2

4

Smoked Salmon Sushi

INGREDIENTS

Serves 4

175 g/6 oz sushi rice
2 tbsp rice vinegar
4 tsp caster sugar
½ tsp salt
2 sheets sushi nori
60 g/2½ oz smoked salmon
¼ cucumber, cut into fine strips

To serve:
wasabi
soy sauce
pickled ginger

TASTY TIP

If wasabi is unavailable, use a little horseradish. If unable to get sushi nori (seaweed sheets), shape the rice into small bite-size oblongs, then drape a piece of smoked salmon over each one and garnish with chives.

1. Rinse the rice thoroughly in cold water, until the water runs clear, then place in a pan with 300 ml/½ pint of water. Bring to the boil and cover with a tight-fitting lid. Reduce to a simmer and cook gently for 10 minutes. Turn the heat off, but keep the pan covered, to allow the rice to steam for a further 10 minutes.

2. In a small saucepan gently heat the rice vinegar, sugar and salt until the sugar has dissolved. When the rice has finished steaming, pour over the vinegar mixture and stir well to mix. Empty the rice out on to a large flat surface (a chopping board or large plate is ideal). Fan the rice to cool and to produce a shinier rice.

3. Lay one sheet of sushi nori on a sushi mat (if you do not have a sushi mat, improvise with a stiff piece of fabric that is a little larger than the sushi nori) and spread with half the cooled rice. Dampen the hands while doing this (this helps to prevent the rice from sticking to the hands). On the nearest edge place half the salmon and half the cucumber strips.

4. Roll up the rice and smoked salmon into a tight Swiss roll-like shape. Dampen the blade of a sharp knife and cut the sushi into slices about 2 cm/¾ inch thick. Repeat with the remaining sushi nori, rice, smoked salmon and cucumber. Serve with wasabi, soy sauce and pickled ginger.

2

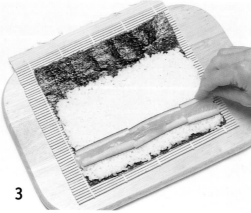

3

4

Italian Baked Tomatoes with Curly Endive & Radicchio

INGREDIENTS

Serves 4

1 tsp olive oil

4 beef tomatoes

salt

50 g/2 oz fresh white breadcrumbs

1 tbsp freshly snipped chives

1 tbsp freshly chopped parsley

125 g/4 oz button mushrooms,
   finely chopped

salt and freshly ground black pepper

25 g/1 oz fresh Parmesan
   cheese, grated

For the salad:

½ curly endive lettuce

½ small piece of radicchio

2 tbsp olive oil

1 tsp balsamic vinegar

salt and freshly ground black pepper

TASTY TIP

As an alternative, try stirring in either 2 tablespoons of tapenade or ready-made pesto into the stuffing mixture. Alternatively, replace the chives with freshly chopped basil.

1 Preheat oven to 190°C/375°F/Gas Mark 5. Lightly oil a baking tray with the teaspoon of oil. Slice the tops off the tomatoes and remove all the tomato flesh and sieve into a large bowl. Sprinkle a little salt inside the tomato shells and then place them upside down on a plate while the filling is prepared.

2 Mix the sieved tomato with the breadcrumbs, fresh herbs and mushrooms and season well with salt and pepper. Place the tomato shells on the prepared baking tray and fill with the tomato and mushroom mixture. Sprinkle the cheese on the top and bake in the preheated oven for 15–20 minutes, until golden brown.

3 Meanwhile, prepare the salad. Arrange the endive and radicchio on individual serving plates and mix the remaining ingredients together in a small bowl to make the dressing. Season to taste.

4 When the tomatoes are cooked, allow to rest for 5 minutes, then place on the prepared plates and drizzle over a little dressing. Serve warm.

1

2

2

Roasted Aubergine Dip with Pitta Strips

INGREDIENTS

Serves 4

4 pitta breads
2 large aubergines
1 garlic clove, peeled
¼ tsp sesame oil
1 tbsp lemon juice
½ tsp ground cumin
salt and freshly ground black pepper
2 tbsp freshly chopped parsley
fresh salad leaves, to serve

FOOD FACT

This dish is a variation on the traditional Arabic dish known as Baba Ganoush, which translates as 'spoilt old man'. As well as being great with pitta strips or bread sticks, this dish is fantastic warmed through and served as a meal accompaniment.

1 Preheat the oven to 180°C/350°F/Gas Mark 4. On a chopping board cut the pitta breads into strips. Spread the bread in a single layer on to a large baking tray.

2 Cook in the preheated oven for 15 minutes until golden and crisp. Leave to cool on a wire cooling rack.

3 Trim the aubergines, rinse lightly and reserve. Heat a griddle pan until almost smoking. Cook the aubergines and garlic for about 15 minutes.

4 Turn the aubergines frequently, until very tender with wrinkled and charred skins. Remove from heat. Leave to cool.

5 When the aubergines are cool enough to handle, cut in half and scoop out the cooked flesh and place in a food processor.

6 Squeeze the softened garlic flesh from the papery skin and add to the aubergine.

7 Blend the aubergine and garlic until smooth, then add the sesame oil, lemon juice and cumin and blend again to mix.

8 Season to taste with salt and pepper, stir in the parsley and serve with the pitta strips and mixed salad leaves.

3

6

7

Moo Shi Pork

INGREDIENTS

Serves 4

175 g/6 oz pork fillet

2 tsp Chinese rice wine or dry sherry

2 tbsp light soy sauce

1 tsp cornflour

25 g/1 oz dried golden needles, soaked and drained

2 tbsp groundnut oil

3 medium eggs, lightly beaten

1 tsp freshly grated root ginger

3 spring onions, trimmed and thinly sliced

150 g/5 oz bamboo shoots, cut into fine strips

salt and freshly ground black pepper

8 mandarin pancakes, steamed

hoisin sauce

sprigs of fresh coriander, to garnish

HELPFUL HINT

Golden needles are dried, unopened lily flowers. They are about 5 cm/2 inches long, have a slightly furry texture and are strongly fragrant. Store in a cool, dark place. They need to be soaked in hot water for about 30 minutes before use, then rinsed and squeezed dry.

1 Cut the pork across the grain into 1 cm/½ inch slices, then cut into thin strips. Place in a bowl with the Chinese rice wine or sherry, soy sauce and cornflour. Mix well and reserve. Trim off the tough ends of the golden needles, then cut in half and reserve.

2 Heat a wok or large frying pan, add 1 tablespoon of the groundnut oil and when hot, add the lightly beaten eggs, and cook for 1 minute, stirring all the time, until scrambled. Remove and reserve. Wipe the wok clean with absorbent kitchen paper.

3 Return the wok to the heat, add the remaining oil and when hot transfer the pork strips from the marinade mixture to the wok, shaking off as much marinade as possible. Stir-fry for 30 seconds, then add the ginger, spring onions and bamboo shoots and pour in the marinade. Stir-fry for 2–3 minutes or until cooked.

4 Return the scrambled eggs to the wok, season to taste with salt and pepper and stir for a few seconds until mixed well and heated through. Divide the mixture between the pancakes, drizzle each with 1 teaspoon of hoisin sauce and roll up. Garnish and serve immediately.

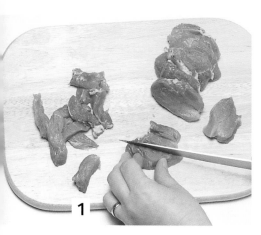

Thai Crab Cakes

INGREDIENTS

Serves 4

200 g/7 oz easy-cook basmati rice
450 ml/³/₄ pint chicken
  stock, heated
200 g/7 oz cooked crab meat
125 g/4 oz cod fillet, skinned
  and minced
5 spring onions, trimmed and
  finely chopped
1 lemon grass stalk, outer leaves
  discarded and finely chopped
1 green chilli, deseeded and
  finely chopped
1 tbsp freshly grated root ginger
1 tbsp freshly chopped coriander
1 tbsp plain flour
1 medium egg
salt and freshly ground black pepper
2 tbsp vegetable oil, for frying

To serve:
sweet chilli dipping sauce
fresh salad leaves

1 Put the rice in a large saucepan and add the hot stock. Bring to the boil, cover and simmer over a low heat, without stirring, for 18 minutes, or until the grains are tender and all the liquid is absorbed.

2 To make the cakes, place the crab meat, fish, spring onions, lemon grass, chilli, ginger, coriander, flour and egg in a food processor. Blend until all the ingredients are mixed thoroughly, then season to taste with salt and pepper. Add the rice to the processor and blend once more, but do not over mix.

3 Remove the mixture from the processor and place on a clean work surface. With damp hands, divide into 12 even-sized patties. Transfer to a plate, cover and chill in the refrigerator for about 30 minutes.

4 Heat the oil in a heavy-based frying pan and cook the crab cakes, 4 at a time, for 3–5 minutes on each side until crisp and golden. Drain on absorbent kitchen paper and serve immediately with a chilli dipping sauce.

1

2

3

Cantonese Chicken Wings

INGREDIENTS

Serves 4

3 tbsp hoisin sauce

2 tbsp dark soy sauce

1 tbsp sesame oil

1 garlic clove, peeled and crushed

2.5 cm/1 inch piece fresh root ginger, peeled and grated

1 tbsp Chinese rice wine or dry sherry

2 tsp chilli bean sauce

2 tsp red or white wine vinegar

2 tbsp soft light brown sugar

900 g/2 lb large chicken wings

50 g/2 oz cashew nuts, chopped

2 spring onions, trimmed and finely chopped

HELPFUL HINT

Chicken wings are regarded as a delicacy in both China and Thailand and are considered one of the tastiest parts of the bird. If you give your butcher advance notice, he will probably sell them to you very cheaply, as they are often trimmed off and discarded when cutting chickens into portions.

1 Preheat the oven to 220°C/425°F/Gas Mark 7, 15 minutes before cooking. Place the hoisin sauce, soy sauce, sesame oil, garlic, ginger, Chinese rice wine or sherry, chilli bean sauce, vinegar and sugar in a small saucepan with 6 tablespoons of water. Bring to the boil, stirring occasionally, then simmer for about 30 seconds. Remove the glaze from the heat.

2 Place the chicken wings in a roasting tin in a single layer. Pour over the glaze and stir until the wings are coated thoroughly.

3 Cover the tin loosely with tinfoil, place in the preheated oven and roast for 25 minutes. Remove the tinfoil, baste the wings and cook for a further 5 minutes.

4 Reduce the oven temperature to 190°C/375°F/Gas Mark 5. Turn the wings over and sprinkle with the chopped cashew nuts and spring onions. Return to the oven and cook for 5 minutes, or until the nuts are lightly browned, the glaze is sticky and the wings are tender. Remove from the oven and leave to stand for 5 minutes before arranging on a warmed platter. Serve immediately with finger bowls and plenty of napkins.

Bruschetta with Pecorino, Garlic & Tomatoes

INGREDIENTS

Serves 4

6 ripe but firm tomatoes

125 g/4 oz pecorino cheese, finely grated

1 tbsp oregano leaves

salt and freshly ground black pepper

3 tbsp olive oil

3 garlic cloves, peeled

8 slices of flat Italian bread, such as focaccia

50 g/2 oz mozzarella cheese

marinated black olives, to serve

1 Preheat grill and line the grill rack with tinfoil just before cooking. Make a small cross in the top of the tomatoes, then place in a small bowl and cover with boiling water. Leave to stand for 2 minutes, then drain and remove the skins. Cut into quarters, remove the seeds, and chop the flesh into small dice.

2 Mix the tomato flesh with the pecorino cheese and 2 teaspoons of the fresh oregano and season to taste with salt and pepper. Add 1 tablespoon of the olive oil and mix thoroughly.

3 Crush the garlic and spread evenly over the slices of bread. Heat 2 tablespoons of the olive oil in a large frying pan and sauté the bread slices until they are crisp and golden.

4 Place the fried bread on a lightly oiled baking tray and spoon on the tomato and cheese topping. Place a little mozzarella on top and place under the preheated grill for 3–4 minutes, until golden and bubbling. Garnish with the remaining oregano, then arrange the bruschettas on a serving plate and serve immediately with the olives.

TASTY TIP

Bitter leaves are excellent with these bruschettas because they help to offset the richness of the cheese and tomato topping. Try a mixture of frisée, radicchio and rocket. If these are unavailable, use a bag of mixed salad leaves.

1

2

3

Crispy Pork Wontons

INGREDIENTS

Serves 4

1 small onion, peeled and
  roughly chopped
2 garlic cloves, peeled and crushed
1 green chilli, deseeded and chopped
2.5 cm/1 inch piece fresh root ginger,
  peeled and roughly chopped
450 g/1 lb lean pork mince
4 tbsp freshly chopped coriander
1 tsp Chinese five-spice powder
salt and freshly ground black pepper
20 wonton wrappers
1 medium egg, lightly beaten
vegetable oil for deep-frying
chilli sauce, to serve

HELPFUL HINT

When frying the wontons, use a deep, heavy based saucepan or special deep-fat fryer fitted with a wire basket. Never fill the pan more than one-third full with oil, then heat over a moderate heat until it reaches the required temperature. Drop a cube of day-old bread into the hot oil. It will turn golden-brown in 45 seconds when the oil is hot enough.

1 Place the onion, garlic, chilli and ginger in a food processor and blend until very finely chopped. Add the pork, coriander and Chinese five-spice powder. Season to taste with salt and pepper, then blend again briefly to mix. Divide the mixture into 20 equal portions and, with floured hands, shape each into a walnut-sized ball.

2 Brush the edges of a wonton wrapper with beaten egg, place a pork ball in the centre, then bring the corners to the centre and pinch together to make a money bag. Repeat with the remaining pork balls and wrappers.

3 Pour sufficient oil into a heavy-based saucepan or deep-fat fryer so that it is one-third full and heat to 180°C/350°F. Deep-fry the wontons in 3 or 4 batches for 3–4 minutes, or until cooked through and golden and crisp. Drain on absorbent kitchen paper. Serve the crispy pork wontons immediately, allowing 5 per person, with some chilli sauce for dipping.

Light Bites

A colourful selection of simple and healthy meals from countries as diverse as Mexico, Thailand and Italy. Whether you require vegetable, fish or meat-based dishes, there is something here to tempt every appetite.

Sicilian Baked Aubergine

INGREDIENTS

Serves 4

1 large aubergine, trimmed
2 celery stalks, trimmed
4 large ripe tomatoes
1 tsp sunflower oil
2 shallots, peeled and
   finely chopped
1½ tsp tomato purée
25 g/1 oz green pitted olives
25 g/1 oz black pitted olives
salt and freshly ground black pepper
1 tbsp white wine vinegar
2 tsp caster sugar
1 tbsp freshly chopped basil,
   to garnish
mixed salad leaves, to serve

FOOD FACT

It has been suggested that foods which are purple in colour, such as aubergines, have particularly powerful antioxidants, which help the body to protect itself from disease and strengthen the organs.

1 Preheat the oven to 200°C/400°F/Gas Mark 6. Cut the aubergine into small cubes and place on an oiled baking tray.

2 Cover the tray with tinfoil and bake in the preheated oven for 15–20 minutes until soft. Reserve, to allow the aubergine to cool.

3 Place the celery and tomatoes in a large bowl and cover with boiling water.

4 Remove the tomatoes from the bowl when their skins begin to peel away. Remove the skins then, deseed and chop the flesh into small pieces.

5 Remove the celery from the bowl of water, finely chop and reserve.

6 Pour the vegetable oil into a non-stick saucepan, add the chopped shallots and fry gently for 2–3 minutes until soft. Add the celery, tomatoes, tomato purée and olives. Season to taste with salt and pepper.

7 Simmer gently for 3–4 minutes. Add the vinegar, sugar and cooled aubergine to the pan and heat gently for 2–3 minutes until all the ingredients are well blended. Reserve to allow the aubergine mixture to cool. When cool, garnish with the chopped basil and serve cold with salad leaves.

1

5

6

Spanish Omelette with Smoked Cod

INGREDIENTS

Serves 3–4

3 tbsp sunflower oil

350 g/12 oz potatoes, peeled and cut
   into 1 cm/½ inch cubes

2 medium onions, peeled and cut
   into wedges

2–4 large garlic cloves, peeled and
   thinly sliced

1 large red pepper, deseeded,
   quartered and thinly sliced

125 g/4 oz smoked cod

salt and freshly ground black pepper

25 g/1 oz butter, melted

1 tbsp double cream

6 medium eggs, beaten

2 tbsp freshly chopped
   flat-leaf parsley

50 g/2 oz mature Cheddar
   cheese, grated

To serve:

crusty bread
tossed green salad, to serve

HELPFUL HINT

For best results, Spanish omelette
should be cooked slowly until set.
Finishing the dish under the grill
gives it a delicious golden look.

1 Heat the oil in a large non-stick heavy-based frying pan, add the
potatoes, onions and garlic and cook gently for 10–15 minutes until
golden brown, then add the red pepper and cook for 3 minutes.

2 Meanwhile, place the fish in a shallow frying pan and cover with
water. Season to taste with salt and pepper and poach gently for
10 minutes. Drain and flake the fish into a bowl, toss in the melted
butter and cream, adjust the seasoning and reserve.

3 When the vegetables are cooked, drain off any excess oil and stir
in the beaten egg with the chopped parsley. Pour the fish mixture
over the top and cook gently for 5 minutes, or until the eggs
become firm.

4 Sprinkle the grated cheese over the top and place the pan under a
preheated hot grill. Cook for 2–3 minutes until the cheese is golden
and bubbling. Carefully slide the omelette onto a large plate and
serve immediately with plenty of bread and salad.

1

2

3

Tempura

INGREDIENTS

Serves 4

For the batter:
200 g/7 oz plain flour
pinch of bicarbonate of soda
1 medium egg yolk

For the prawns & vegetables:
8–12 raw king size prawns
1 carrot, peeled
125 g/4 oz button mushrooms, wiped
1 green pepper, deseeded
1 small aubergine, trimmed
1 onion, peeled
125 g/4 oz French beans
125 ml/4 fl oz sesame oil
300 ml/½ pint vegetable oil for
  deep frying

To serve:
soy sauce
chilli dipping sauce

FOOD FACT
The bicarbonate of soda in the batter helps it to rise quickly when it hits the hot oil and then helps to keep the batter crisp once it is drained.

1 Sift the flour and bicarbonate of soda into a mixing bowl. Blend 450 ml/¾ pint water and the egg yolk together, then gradually whisk into the flour mixture until a smooth batter is formed.

2 Peel the prawns, leaving the tails intact, de-vein, then rinse lightly and pat dry with absorbent kitchen paper and reserve. Slice the carrot thinly then, using small pastry cutters, cut out fancy shapes. Cut the mushrooms in half, if large, and cut the pepper into chunks. Slice the aubergine, then cut into chunks, together with the onion, and finally trim the French beans.

3 Pour the sesame oil and the vegetable oil into a large wok and heat to 180°C/350°F, or until a small spoonful of the batter dropped into the oil sizzles and cooks on impact.

4 Dip the prawns and vegetables into the reserved batter (no more than 8 pieces at a time) and stir until lightly coated. Cook for 3 minutes, turning occasionally during cooking, or until evenly golden. Using a slotted spoon, transfer the prawns and vegetables onto absorbent kitchen paper and drain well. Keep warm. Repeat with the remaining ingredients. Serve immediately with soy sauce and chilli dipping sauce.

Risi e Bisi

INGREDIENTS

Serves 4

700 g/1½ lb young peas in
   pods or 175 g/6 oz frozen petits
   pois, thawed
25 g/1 oz unsalted butter
1 tsp olive oil
3 rashers pancetta or unsmoked back
   bacon, chopped
1 small onion, peeled and
   finely chopped
1 garlic clove, peeled and
   finely chopped
1.3 litres/2¼ pints vegetable stock
pinch of caster sugar
1 tsp lemon juice
1 bay leaf
200 g/7 oz Arborio rice
3 tbsp freshly chopped parsley
50 g/2 oz Parmesan cheese,
   finely grated
salt and freshly ground black pepper

To garnish:
sprig of fresh parsley
julienne strips of orange rind

1   Shell the peas, if using fresh ones. Melt the butter and olive oil together in a large, heavy-based saucepan. Add the chopped pancetta or bacon, the chopped onion and garlic and gently fry for about 10 minutes, or until the onion is softened and is just beginning to colour.

2   Pour in the vegetable stock, then add the caster sugar, lemon juice and bay leaf. Add the fresh peas if using. Bring the mixture to a fast boil.

3   Add the rice, stir and simmer, uncovered, for about 20 minutes, or until the rice is tender. Occasionally, stir the mixture gently while it cooks. If using frozen petits pois, stir them into the rice about 2 minutes before the end of the cooking time.

4   When the rice is cooked, remove the bay leaf and discard. Stir in 2½ tablespoons of the chopped parsley and the grated Parmesan cheese. Season to taste with salt and pepper.

5   Transfer the rice to a large serving dish. Garnish with the remaining chopped parsley, a sprig of fresh parsley and julienne strips of orange rind. Serve immediately while piping hot.

Singapore Noodles

INGREDIENTS

Serves 4

225 g/8 oz thin round egg noodles

3 tbsp groundnut or vegetable oil

125 g/4 oz field mushrooms, wiped
and thinly sliced

2.5 cm/1 inch piece root ginger,
peeled and finely chopped

1 red chilli, deseeded and thinly sliced

1 red pepper, deseeded and
thinly sliced

2 garlic cloves, peeled and crushed

1 medium courgette, cut in half
lengthways and diagonally sliced

4-6 spring onions, trimmed and
thinly sliced

50 g/2 oz frozen garden peas, thawed

1 tbsp curry paste

2 tbsp tomato ketchup

salt or soy sauce

125 g/4 oz beansprouts, rinsed and
drained

To garnish:

sesame seeds

fresh coriander leaves

1 Bring a large pan of lightly salted water to a rolling boil. Add the
noodles and cook according to the packet instructions, or until
'al dente'. Drain thoroughly and toss with 1 tablespoon of the oil.

2 Heat the remaining oil in a wok or large frying pan over high heat.
Add the mushrooms, ginger, chilli and red pepper and stir-fry for
2 minutes. Add the garlic, courgettes, spring onions and garden
peas and stir lightly.

3 Push the vegetables to one side and add the curry paste, tomato
ketchup and about 125 ml/4 fl oz hot water. Season to taste with
salt or a few drops of soy sauce and allow to boil vigorously, stirring,
until the paste is smooth.

4 Stir the reserved egg noodles and the beansprouts into the
vegetable mixture and stir-fry until coated with the paste and
thoroughly heated through. Season with more soy sauce if
necessary, then turn into a large warmed serving bowl or spoon
on to individual plates. Garnish with sesame seeds and coriander
leaves. Serve immediately.

Melanzane Parmigiana

INGREDIENTS

Serves 4

900 g/2 lb aubergines
salt and freshly ground black pepper
5 tbsp olive oil
1 red onion, peeled and chopped
½ tsp mild paprika pepper
150 ml/¼ pint dry red wine
150 ml/¼ pint vegetable stock
400 g can chopped tomatoes
1 tsp tomato purée
1 tbsp freshly chopped oregano
175 g/6 oz mozzarella cheese,
   thinly sliced
40 g/1½ oz Parmesan cheese,
   coarsely grated
sprig of fresh basil, to garnish

1. Preheat oven to 200°C/400°F/Gas Mark 6, 15 minutes before cooking. Cut the aubergines lengthways into thin slices. Sprinkle with salt and leave to drain in a colander over a bowl for 30 minutes.

2. Meanwhile, heat 1 tablespoon of the olive oil in a saucepan and fry the onion for 10 minutes, until softened. Add the paprika and cook for 1 minute. Stir in the wine, stock, tomatoes and tomato purée. Simmer, uncovered, for 25 minutes, or until fairly thick. Stir in the oregano and season to taste with salt and pepper. Remove from the heat.

3. Rinse the aubergine slices thoroughly under cold water and pat dry on absorbent kitchen paper. Heat 2 tablespoons of the oil in a griddle pan and cook the aubergines in batches, for 3 minutes on each side, until golden. Drain well on absorbent kitchen paper.

4. Pour half of the tomato sauce into the base of a large ovenproof dish. Cover with half the aubergine slices, then top with the mozzarella. Cover with the remaining aubergine slices and pour over the remaining tomato sauce. Sprinkle with the grated Parmesan cheese.

5. Bake in the preheated oven for 30 minutes, or until the aubergines are tender and the sauce is bubbling. Garnish with a sprig of fresh basil and cool for a few minutes before serving.

HELPFUL HINT

Salting the aubergine draws out some of the moisture, so you'll need less oil when frying.

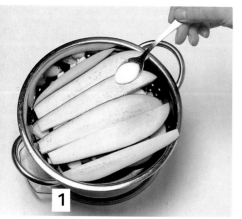

1

3

4

Fettucini with Roasted Beetroot & Rocket

INGREDIENTS

Serves 4

350 g/12 oz raw baby
 beetroot, unpeeled
1 garlic clove, peeled and crushed
½ tsp finely grated orange rind
1 tbsp orange juice
1 tsp lemon juice
2 tbsp walnut oil
salt and freshly ground black pepper
350 g/12 oz dried fettucini
75 g/3 oz rocket leaves
125 g/4 oz Dolcelatte cheese, cut into
 small cubes

HELPFUL HINT

Many large supermarkets sell raw beetroot, but baby beetroot may be more readily available from specialist or ethnic greengrocers. Look for beetroot with the leaves attached. The bulbs should be firm without any soft spots and the leaves should not be wilted.

1. Preheat oven to 150°C/300°F/Gas Mark 2, 10 minutes before cooking. Wrap the beetroot individually in tinfoil and bake for 1–1½ hours, or until tender. (Test by opening one of the parcels and scraping the skin away from the stem end – it should come off very easily.)

2. Leave the beetroot until cool enough to handle, then peel and cut each beetroot into 6–8 wedges, depending on the size. Mix the garlic, orange rind and juice, lemon juice, walnut oil and salt and pepper together, then drizzle over the beetroot and toss to coat well.

3. Meanwhile, bring a large saucepan of lightly salted water to the boil. Cook the pasta for 10 minutes, or until 'al dente'.

4. Drain the pasta thoroughly, then add the warm beetroot, rocket leaves and Dolcelatte cheese. Quickly and gently toss together, then divide between serving bowls and serve immediately before the rocket wilts.

1

2

4

Panzerotti

INGREDIENTS

Serves 16

450 g/1 lb strong white flour
pinch of salt
1 tsp easy-blend dried yeast
2 tbsp olive oil
300 ml/½ pint warm water
fresh rocket leaves, to serve

For the filling:

1 tbsp olive oil
1 small red onion, peeled and
 finely chopped
2 garlic cloves, peeled and crushed
½ yellow pepper, deseeded
 and chopped
1 small courgette, about 75 g/
 3 oz, trimmed and chopped
50 g/2 oz black olives, pitted
 and quartered
125 g/4 oz mozzarella cheese, cut
 into tiny cubes
salt and freshly ground black pepper
5–6 tbsp tomato purée
1 tsp dried mixed herbs
oil for deep-frying

1 Sift the flour and salt into a bowl. Stir in the yeast. Make a well in the centre. Add the oil and the warm water and mix to a soft dough. Knead on a lightly floured surface until smooth and elastic. Put in an oiled bowl, cover and leave in a warm place to rise while making the filling.

2 To make the filling, heat the oil in a frying pan and cook the onion for 5 minutes. Add the garlic, yellow pepper and courgette. Cook for about 5 minutes, or until the vegetables are tender. Tip into a bowl and leave to cool slightly. Stir in the olives, mozzarella cheese and season to taste with salt and pepper.

3 Briefly reknead the dough. Divide into 16 equal pieces. Roll out each to a circle about 10 cm/4 inches. Mix together the tomato purée and dried herbs, then spread about 1 teaspoon on each circle, leaving a 2 cm/¾ inch border around the edge.

4 Divide the filling equally between the circles, it will seem a small amount, but if you overfill, they will leak during cooking. Brush the edges with water, then fold in half to enclose the filling. Press to seal, then crimp the edges.

5 Heat the oil in a deep-fat fryer to 180°C/350°F. Deep-fry the panzerotti in batches for 3 minutes, or until golden. Drain on absorbent kitchen paper and keep warm in a low oven until ready to serve with fresh rocket.

1

2

4

Thai Prawn & Rice Noodle Salad

INGREDIENTS

Serves 4

75 g/3 oz rice vermicelli
175 g/6 oz mangetout, cut
  in half crossways
½ cucumber, peeled, deseeded
  and diced
2–3 spring onions, trimmed and
  thinly sliced diagonally
16–20 large cooked tiger prawns,
  peeled with tails left on
2 tbsp chopped unsalted peanuts
  or cashews

For the dressing:

4 tbsp freshly squeezed lime juice
3 tbsp Thai fish sauce
1 tbsp sugar
2.5 cm/1 inch piece fresh root ginger,
  peeled and finely chopped
1 red chilli, deseeded and thinly sliced
3–4 tbsp freshly chopped coriander
  or mint

To garnish:

lime wedges
sprigs of fresh mint

1 Place the vermicelli in a bowl and pour over hot water to cover. Leave to stand for 5 minutes or until softened. Drain, rinse, then drain again and reserve.

2 Meanwhile, mix all the dressing ingredients in a large bowl until well blended and the sugar has dissolved. Reserve.

3 Bring a medium saucepan of water to the boil. Add the mangetout, return to the boil and cook for 30–50 seconds. Drain, refresh under cold running water, drain again and reserve.

4 Stir the cucumber, spring onions and all but 4 of the prawns into the dressing until coated lightly. Add the mangetout and noodles and toss until all the ingredients are mixed evenly.

5 Spoon the noodle salad on to warmed individual plates. Sprinkle with peanuts or cashews and garnish each dish with a reserved prawn, a lime wedge and a sprig of mint.

2

2

4

Warm Lobster Salad

INGREDIENTS

Serves 4

1 orange

50 g/2 oz granulated sugar

2 Cos lettuce hearts, shredded

1 small avocado, peeled and sliced

½ cucumber, peeled, deseeded
   and thinly sliced

1 ripe mango, peeled, stoned
   and thinly sliced

1 tbsp butter or vegetable oil

1 large lobster, meat removed and cut
   into bite-sized pieces

2 tbsp Thai or Italian basil leaves

4 large cooked prawns, peeled with
   tails left on, to garnish

For the dressing:

1 tbsp vegetable oil

4–6 spring onions, trimmed and
   sliced into 5 cm/2 inch pieces

2.5 cm/1 inch piece fresh root ginger,
   peeled and grated

1 garlic clove, peeled and crushed

grated zest of 1 lime

juice of 2–3 small limes

2 tbsp Thai fish sauce

1 tbsp brown sugar

1–2 tsp sweet chilli sauce

1 tbsp sesame oil

1 With a sharp knife, cut the orange rind into thin julienne strips, then cook in boiling water for 2 minutes.

2 Drain the orange strips, then plunge into cold running water, drain and return to the saucepan with the sugar and 1 cm/½ inch water. Simmer until soft, then add 1 tablespoon of cold water to stop cooking. Remove from the heat and reserve. Arrange the lettuce on 4 large plates and arrange the avocado, cucumber and mango slices over the lettuce.

3 Heat a wok or large frying pan, add the butter or oil and when hot, but not sizzling, add the lobster and stir-fry for 1–2 minutes or until heated through. Remove and drain on absorbent kitchen paper.

4 To make the dressing, heat the vegetable oil in a wok, then add the spring onions, ginger and garlic and stir-fry for 1 minute. Add the lime zest, lime juice, fish sauce, sugar and chilli sauce. Stir until the sugar dissolves. Remove from the heat, add the sesame oil with the orange rind and liquor.

5 Arrange the lobster meat over the salad and drizzle with dressing. Sprinkle with basil leaves, garnish with prawns and serve immediately.

Thai Spring Rolls with Noodles & Dipping Sauce

INGREDIENTS

Makes about 30

50 g/2 oz dried rice vermicelli
1 carrot, peeled and cut
   into matchsticks
50 g/2 oz mangetout peas, thinly
   shredded lengthways
3 spring onions, trimmed and
   finely chopped
125 g/4 oz peeled prawns,
   thawed if frozen
2 garlic cloves, peeled and crushed
1 tsp sesame oil
2 tbsp light soy sauce
1 tsp chilli sauce
200 g/7 oz filo pastry, cut into
   15 cm/6 inch squares
1 medium egg white, lightly beaten
vegetable oil for deep frying
sprigs of fresh coriander, to garnish
sweet chilli sauce, for dipping

HELPFUL HINT

If available, use spring roll wrappers instead of filo pastry. Buy the larger sized ones and follow the recipe from step 2.

1 Cook the rice vermicelli according to the packet directions, then drain thoroughly. Roughly chop and reserve. Bring a saucepan of lightly salted water to the boil and blanch the carrot and mangetout peas for 1 minute. Drain and refresh under cold water, then drain again and pat dry on absorbent kitchen paper. Mix together with the noodles. Add the spring onions, prawns, garlic, sesame oil, soy sauce and chilli sauce and reserve.

2 Fold the filo pastry squares in half diagonally to form triangles. Lay a triangle with the fold facing you and place a spoonful of the mixture in the centre. Roll over the long end of the wrapper to enclose the filling, then bring over the corners to enclose the ends of the roll. Brush the point of the spring roll furthest from you with a little beaten egg white and continue rolling to seal.

3 Fill a wok about a third full with vegetable oil and heat to 190°C/375°F, or until a cube of bread browns in 30 seconds. Fry the spring rolls, 4 or 5 at a time, for 1–2 minutes, or until golden and crisp. Drain on absorbent kitchen paper. Fry the remaining spring rolls in batches. Garnish with sprigs of coriander and serve hot with the dark soy sauce and sweet chilli sauce.

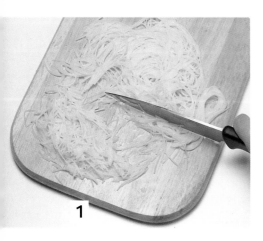

1

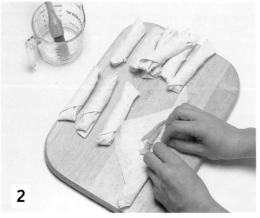

2

3

Thai Green Fragrant Mussels

INGREDIENTS

Serves 4

2 kg/4¹/₂ lb fresh mussels
4 tbsp olive oil
2 garlic cloves, peeled and
    finely sliced
3 tbsp fresh root ginger, peeled and
    finely sliced
3 lemon grass stalks, outer leaves
    discarded and finely sliced
1–3 red or green chillies, deseeded
    and chopped
1 green pepper, deseeded and diced
5 spring onions, trimmed and
    finely sliced
3 tbsp freshly chopped coriander
1 tbsp sesame oil
juice of 3 limes
400 ml can coconut milk
warm crusty bread, to serve

HELPFUL HINT

Mussels and other shellfish are often eaten raw in Thailand. The less they are cooked the better, as they will toughen if overcooked and lose their fresh sea flavour. Buy mussels no more than 24 hours before you need them, so that they are really fresh.

1 Scrub the mussels under cold running water, removing any barnacles and beards. Discard any that have broken or damaged shells or are opened and do not close when tapped gently.

2 Heat a wok or large frying pan, add the oil and when hot, add the mussels. Shake gently and cook for 1 minute, then add the garlic, ginger, sliced lemon grass, chillies, green pepper, spring onions, 2 tablespoons of the chopped coriander and the sesame oil.

3 Stir-fry over a medium heat for 3–4 minutes, or until the mussels are cooked and have opened. Discard any mussels that remain unopened.

4 Pour the lime juice with the coconut milk into the wok and bring to the boil. Tip the mussels and the cooking liquor into warmed individual bowls. Sprinkle with the remaining chopped coriander and serve immediately with warm crusty bread.

Spiced Tomato Pilau

INGREDIENTS

Serves 2–3

225 g/8 oz basmati rice
40 g/1½ oz unsalted butter
4 green cardamom pods
2 star anise
4 whole cloves
10 black peppercorns
5 cm/2 inch piece cinnamon stick
1 large red onion, peeled and
   finely sliced
175 g/6 oz canned chopped tomatoes
salt and freshly ground black pepper
sprigs of fresh coriander, to garnish

1 Wash the rice in several changes of water until the water remains relatively clear. Drain the rice and cover with fresh water. Leave to soak for 30 minutes. Drain well and reserve.

2 Heat the wok, then melt the butter and add the cardamoms, star anise, cloves, black peppercorns and the cinnamon stick. Cook gently for 30 seconds. Increase the heat and add the onion. Stir-fry for 7–8 minutes until tender and starting to brown. Add the drained rice and cook a further 2–3 minutes.

3 Sieve the tomatoes and mix with sufficient warm water to make 450 ml/16 fl oz. Pour this into the wok, season to taste with salt and pepper and bring to the boil.

4 Cover, reduce the heat to very low and cook for 10 minutes. Remove the wok from the heat and leave covered for a further 10 minutes. Do not lift the lid during cooking or resting. Finally, uncover and mix well with a fork, heat for 1 minute, then garnish with the sprigs of fresh coriander and serve immediately.

HELPFUL HINT

The whole spices in this recipe are not meant to be eaten. Remove them before serving.

1

2

3

Crispy Noodle Salad

INGREDIENTS

Serves 4

2 tbsp sunflower seeds

2 tbsp pumpkin seeds

50 g/2 oz rice vermicelli or
  stir-fry noodles

175 g/6 oz unsalted butter

2 tbsp sesame seeds, lightly toasted

125 g/4 oz red cabbage, trimmed
  and shredded

1 orange pepper, deseeded and
  finely chopped

125 g/4 oz button mushrooms, wiped
  and quartered

2 spring onions, trimmed and
  finely chopped

salt and freshly ground black pepper

shredded pickled sushi ginger,
  to garnish

1 Preheat the oven to 200°C/400°F/Gas Mark 6, then sprinkle the sunflower and pumpkin seeds on a baking sheet. Toast in the oven, stirring occasionally, for 10–15 minutes or until lightly toasted. Remove from the oven and leave to cool.

2 Crush the rice vermicelli into small pieces (this is easiest in a plastic bag or while the noodles are still in the packet), and reserve. Melt the butter in a small saucepan and leave to cool for a few minutes. Pour the clear yellow liquid carefully into a bowl, leaving behind the white milky solids. Discard the milky solids.

3 Heat the yellow, clarified butter in a wok and fry the crushed noodles in batches until browned, stirring constantly and gently. Remove the fried noodles as they cook, using a slotted spoon, and drain on absorbent kitchen paper. Transfer the noodles to a bowl and add the toasted seeds.

4 Mix together the red cabbage, orange pepper, button mushrooms and spring onions in a large bowl and season to taste with salt and pepper. Just before serving, add the noodles and seeds to the salad and mix gently. Garnish with a little sushi ginger and serve.

HELPFUL HINT

Do not leave the salad to stand after adding the crispy noodles, as the moisture in the vegetables will cause them to wilt and soften.

1

2

3

Chicken & Lamb Satay

INGREDIENTS

Makes 16

225 g/8 oz skinless, boneless chicken
225 g/8 oz lean lamb

For the marinade:
1 small onion, peeled and
  finely chopped
2 garlic cloves, peeled and crushed
2.5 cm/1 inch piece fresh root ginger,
  peeled and grated
4 tbsp soy sauce
1 tsp ground coriander
2 tsp dark brown sugar
2 tbsp lime juice
1 tbsp vegetable oil

For the peanut sauce:
300 ml/½ pint coconut milk
4 tbsp crunchy peanut butter
1 tbsp Thai fish sauce
1 tsp lime juice
1 tbsp chilli powder
1 tbsp brown sugar
salt and freshly ground black pepper

To garnish:
sprigs of fresh coriander
lime wedges

1 Preheat the grill just before cooking. Soak the bamboo skewers for 30 minutes before required. Cut the chicken and lamb into thin strips, about 7.5 cm/3 inches long and place in 2 shallow dishes. Blend all the marinade ingredients together, then pour half over the chicken and half over the lamb. Stir until lightly coated, then cover with clingfilm and leave to marinate in the refrigerator for at least 2 hours, turning occasionally.

2 Remove the chicken and lamb from the marinade and thread on to the skewers. Reserve the marinade. Cook under the preheated grill for 8–10 minutes or until cooked, turning and brushing with the marinade.

3 Meanwhile, make the peanut sauce. Blend the coconut milk with the peanut butter, fish sauce, lime juice, chilli powder and sugar. Pour into a saucepan and cook gently for 5 minutes, stirring occasionally, then season to taste with salt and pepper. Garnish with coriander sprigs and lime wedges and serve the satays with the prepared sauce.

1

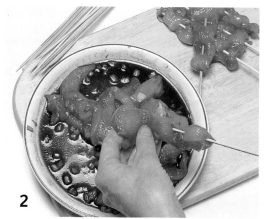

2

3

Mediterranean Chowder

INGREDIENTS

Serves 6

1 tbsp olive oil

1 tbsp butter

1 large onion, peeled and finely sliced

4 celery stalks, trimmed and
   thinly sliced

2 garlic cloves, peeled and crushed

1 bird's-eye chilli, deseeded and
   finely chopped

1 tbsp plain flour

225 g/8 oz potatoes, peeled and diced

600 ml/1 pint fish or vegetable stock

700 g/1½ lb whiting or cod fillet cut
   into 2.5 cm/1 inch cubes

2 tbsp freshly chopped parsley

125 g/4 oz large peeled prawns

198 g can sweetcorn, drained

salt and freshly ground black pepper

150 ml/¼ pint single cream

1 tbsp freshly snipped chives

warm, crusty bread, to serve

1 Heat the oil and butter together in a large saucepan, add the onion, celery and garlic and cook gently for 2–3 minutes until softened. Add the chilli and stir in the flour. Cook, stirring, for a further minute.

2 Add the potatoes to the saucepan with the stock. Bring to the boil, cover and simmer for 10 minutes. Add the fish cubes to the saucepan with the chopped parsley and cook for a further 5–10 minutes, or until the fish and potatoes are just tender.

3 Stir in the peeled prawns and sweetcorn and season to taste with salt and pepper. Pour in the cream and adjust the seasoning, if necessary.

4 Scatter the snipped chives over the top of the chowder. Ladle into 6 large bowls and serve immediately with plenty of warm crusty bread.

Light Ratatouille

INGREDIENTS

Serves 4

1 red pepper

2 courgettes, trimmed

1 small aubergine, trimmed

1 onion, peeled

2 ripe tomatoes

50 g/2 oz button mushrooms, wiped
  and halved or quartered

200 ml/7 fl oz tomato juice

1 tbsp freshly chopped basil

salt and freshly ground black pepper

1   Deseed the peppers, remove the membrane with a small sharp knife and cut into small dice. Thickly slice the courgettes and cut the aubergine into small dice. Slice the onion into rings.

2   Place the tomatoes in boiling water until their skins begin to peel away.

3   Remove the skins from the tomatoes, cut into quarters and remove the seeds.

4   Place all the vegetables in a saucepan with the tomato juice and basil. Season to taste with salt and pepper.

5   Bring to the boil, cover and simmer for 15 minutes or until the vegetables are tender.

6   Remove the vegetables with a slotted spoon and arrange in a serving dish.

7   Bring the liquid in the pan to the boil and boil for 20 seconds until it is slightly thickened. Season the sauce to taste with salt and pepper.

8   Pass the sauce through a sieve to remove some of the seeds and pour over the vegetables. Serve the ratatouille hot or cold.

TASTY TIP

This dish would be perfect, served as an accompaniment. It is also delicious in an omelette or as a jacket potato filling.

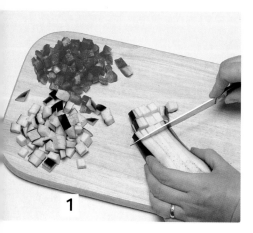

1

4

6

Potato Gnocchi with Pesto Sauce

INGREDIENTS

Serves 6

900 g/2 lb floury potatoes
40 g/1½ oz butter
1 medium egg, beaten
225 g/8 oz plain flour
1 tsp salt
freshly ground black pepper
25 g/1 oz Parmesan cheese, shaved
rocket salad, to serve

For the pesto sauce:

50 g/2 oz fresh basil leaves
1 large garlic clove, peeled
2 tbsp pine nuts
125 ml/4 fl oz olive oil
40 g/1½ oz Parmesan cheese, grated

1. Cook the potatoes in their skins in boiling water for 20 minutes, or until tender. Drain and peel. While still warm, push the potatoes through a fine sieve into a bowl. Stir in the butter, egg, 175 g/6 oz of the flour, the salt and pepper.

2. Sift the remaining flour onto a board or work surface, add the potato mixture. Gently knead in enough flour until a soft, slightly sticky dough is formed.

3. With floured hands, break off portions of the dough and roll into 2.5 cm/1 inch thick ropes. Cut into 2 cm/¾ inch lengths. Lightly press each piece against the inner prongs of a fork. Put on a tray covered with a floured tea towel and chill in the refrigerator for about 30 minutes.

4. To make the pesto sauce, put the basil, garlic, pine nuts and oil in a processor and blend until smooth and creamy. Turn into a bowl and stir in the Parmesan cheese. Season to taste.

5. Cooking in several batches, drop the gnocchi into a saucepan of barely simmering salted water. Cook for 3–4 minutes, or until they float to the surface. Remove with a slotted spoon and keep warm in a covered oiled baking dish in a low oven.

6. Add the gnocchi to the pesto sauce and toss gently to coat. Serve immediately, scattered with the Parmesan cheese and accompanied by a rocket salad.

HELPFUL HINT

Use a vegetable peeler to pare the Parmesan cheese into decorative thin curls.

1

3

5

Calypso Rice with Curried Bananas

INGREDIENTS

Serves 4

2 tbsp sunflower oil

1 medium onion, peeled and
   finely chopped

1 garlic clove, peeled and crushed

1 red chilli, deseeded and
   finely chopped

1 red pepper, deseeded and chopped

225 g/8 oz basmati rice

juice of 1 lime

350 ml/12 fl oz vegetable stock

200 g can black-eye beans, drained
   and rinsed

2 tbsp freshly chopped parsley

salt and freshly ground black pepper

sprigs of coriander, to garnish

For the curried bananas:

4 green bananas

2 tbsp sunflower oil

2 tsp mild curry paste

200 ml/7 fl oz coconut milk

1. Heat the oil in a large frying pan and gently cook the onion, for 10 minutes until soft. Add the garlic, chilli and red pepper and cook for 2–3 minutes.

2. Rinse the rice under cold running water, then add to the pan and stir. Pour in the lime juice and stock, bring to the boil, cover and simmer for 12–15 minutes, or until the rice is tender and the stock is absorbed.

3. Stir in the black-eye beans and chopped parsley and season to taste with salt and pepper. Leave to stand, covered, for 5 minutes before serving, to allow the beans to warm through.

4. While the rice is cooking, make the curried green bananas. Remove the skins from the bananas – they may need to be cut off with a sharp knife. Slice the flesh thickly. Heat the oil in a frying pan and cook the bananas, in 2 batches, for 2–3 minutes, or until lightly browned.

5. Pour the coconut milk into the pan and stir in the curry paste.

6. Add the banana slices to the coconut milk and simmer, uncovered, over a low heat for 8–10 minutes, or until the bananas are very soft and the coconut milk slightly reduced.

7. Spoon the rice onto warmed serving plates, garnish with coriander and serve immediately with the curried bananas.

3

4

5

Wild Rice Dolmades

INGREDIENTS

Serves 4

6 tbsp olive oil
25 g/1 oz pine nuts
175 g/6 oz mushrooms, wiped and finely chopped
4 spring onions, trimmed and finely chopped
1 garlic clove, peeled and crushed
50 g/2 oz cooked wild rice
2 tsp freshly chopped dill
2 tsp freshly chopped mint
salt and freshly ground black pepper
16–24 prepared medium vine leaves
about 300 ml/½ pint vegetable stock

To garnish:
lemon wedges
sprigs of fresh dill

HELPFUL HINT

Fresh vine leaves are available in early summer and should be blanched for 2–3 minutes in boiling water. Vine leaves preserved in brine can be found all year round in supermarkets – soak in warm water for 20 minutes before using.

1 Heat 1 tbsp of the oil in a frying pan and gently cook the pine nuts for 2–3 minutes, stirring frequently, until golden. Remove from the pan and reserve.

2 Add 1½ tablespoons of oil to the pan and gently cook the mushrooms, spring onions and garlic for 7–8 minutes until very soft. Stir in the rice, herbs, salt and pepper.

3 Put a heaped teaspoon of stuffing in the centre of each leaf (if the leaves are small, put 2 together, overlapping slightly). Fold over the stalk end, then the sides and roll up to make a neat parcel. Continue until all the stuffing is used.

4 Arrange the stuffed vine leaves close together seam-side down in a large saucepan, drizzling each with a little of the remaining oil – there will be several layers. Pour over just enough stock to cover.

5 Put an inverted plate over the dolmades to stop them unrolling during cooking. Bring to the boil, then simmer very gently for 3 minutes. Cool in the saucepan.

6 Transfer the dolmades to a serving dish. Cover and chill in the refrigerator before serving. Sprinkle with the pine nuts and garnish with lemon and dill. Serve.

1

2

3

French Onion Tart

INGREDIENTS

Serves 4

Quick flaky pastry:
125 g/4 oz butter
175 g/6 oz plain flour
pinch of salt

For the filling:
2 tbsp olive oil
4 large onions, peeled and
 thinly sliced
3 tbsp white wine vinegar
2 tbsp muscovado sugar
a little beaten egg or milk
175 g/6 oz Cheddar
 cheese, grated
salt and freshly ground black pepper

1 Preheat the oven to 200°C/400°F/Gas Mark 6. Place the butter in the freezer for 30 minutes. Sift the flour and salt into a large bowl. Coarsely grate the partially frozen butter, dipping the butter in the flour every now and again as it makes it easier to grate.

2 Mix the butter into the flour, using a knife, making sure all the butter is coated thoroughly with flour. Add 2 tablespoons of cold water and continue to mix, using your hands to bring the mixture together. Add a little more water if needed to leave a clean bowl. Place the pastry in a polythene bag and chill in the refrigerator for 30 minutes.

3 Heat the oil in a large frying pan, then fry the onions for 10 minutes, stirring occasionally until softened.

4 Stir in the white wine vinegar and sugar. Increase the heat and stir frequently for another 4–5 minutes until the onions turn a deep caramel colour. Cook for another 5 minutes, then reserve to cool.

5 On a lightly floured surface, roll out the pastry to a 35.5 cm/14 inch circle. Move the circle on to a baking sheet.

6 Sprinkle half the cheese over the pastry, leaving a 5 cm/2 inch border around the edge, then add the caramelised onions.

7 Fold the uncovered pastry edges over the edge of the filling to form a rim and brush the rim with beaten egg or milk.

8 Season to taste with salt and pepper. Sprinkle over the remaining Cheddar and bake for 20–25 minutes. Transfer to a large plate and serve immediately.

TASTY TIP
For a milder, nutty taste, substitute the Cheddar cheese for Gruyère and grate a little nutmeg over the layer of cheese in step 7.

1

5

6

Parsnip Tatin

INGREDIENTS

Serves 4

1 quantity shortcrust pastry

For the filling:

50 g/2 oz butter
8 small parsnips, peeled and halved
1 tbsp brown sugar
75 ml/3 fl oz apple juice

FOOD FACT

In many parts of Europe, parsnips are unpopular. Indeed, in Italy they feed them to the pigs. However, parsnips are great winter warmers especially when mashed with potatoes.

TASTY TIP

This dish is delicious served warm with a Greek salad. Feta cheese is one of the main ingredients in Greek salad and because of its salty taste, it tastes particularly good with the creamy flavour of parsnips in this recipe.

1. Preheat the oven to 200°C/400°F/Gas Mark 6. Heat the butter in a 20.5 cm/8 inch frying pan.

2. Add the parsnips, arranging the cut-side down with the narrow ends towards the centre.

3. Sprinkle the parsnips with sugar and cook for 15 minutes, turning halfway through until golden.

4. Add the apple juice and bring to the boil. Remove the pan from the heat.

5. On a lightly floured surface, roll the pastry out to a size slightly larger than the frying pan.

6. Position the pastry over the parsnips and press down slightly to enclose the parsnips.

7. Bake in the preheated oven for 20–25 minutes until the parsnips and pastry are golden.

8. Invert a warm serving plate over the pan and carefully turn the pan over to flip the tart on to the plate. Serve immediately.

3

6

8

Avocado, Bean & Steak Salad

INGREDIENTS

Serves 4

350 g/12 oz tender steak, such as
   sirloin or filet
4 garlic cloves, chopped
juice of 1 lime
4 tbsp extra-virgin olive oil
1 tbsp white or red wine vinegar
$\frac{1}{4}$ tsp mild chilli powder
$\frac{1}{4}$ tsp ground cumin
$\frac{1}{2}$ tsp paprika
pinch of sugar (optional)
5 spring onions, thinly sliced
about 200 g/7 oz crisp lettuce leaves,
   such as Cos, or mixed herb leaves
400 g/14 oz can pinto, black or red
   kidney beans, drained
1 avocado, stoned (pitted), sliced and
   tossed with a little lime juice
2 ripe tomatoes, diced
$\frac{1}{4}$ fresh green or red chilli, chopped
3 tbsp chopped fresh coriander
225 g/8 oz can sweetcorn, drained
generous handful of crisp tortilla
   chips, broken into pieces
salt and pepper

1 Place the steak in a non-metallic dish with the garlic and half the lime and olive oil. Season with salt and pepper, then leave to marinate.

2 To make the dressing, combine the remaining lime juice and olive oil with the vinegar, chilli powder, cumin and paprika. Add a pinch of sugar to taste. Set aside.

3 Pan fry the steak, or cook under a preheated grill, until browned on the outside and cooked to your liking in the middle. Remove from the pan, cut into strips and reserve; keep warm or allow to cool.

4 Toss the spring onions with the lettuce and arrange on a serving platter. Pour about half the dressing over the leaves, then arrange the sweetcorn, beans, avocado and tomatoes over the top. Sprinkle with the chilli and coriander.

5 Arrange the steak and the tortilla chips on top, pour over the rest of the dressing, and serve at once.

3

4

5

Potatoes with Goat's Cheese & Chipotle Cream

INGREDIENTS

Serves 4

1.25 kg/2 lb 12 oz baking potatoes, peeled and cut into chunks
pinch of salt
pinch of sugar
200 ml/7 fl oz crème fraîche
120 ml/4 fl oz vegetable or chicken stock
3 garlic cloves, finely chopped
a few shakes of bottled chipotle salsa, or ½ dried chipotle, reconstituted, deseeded and thinly sliced
225 g/8 oz goat's cheese, sliced
175 g/6 oz mozzarella or Cheddar cheese, grated
50 g/¾ oz Parmesan or pecorino cheese, grated
salt

1 Put the potatoes in a pan of water with the salt and sugar. Bring to the boil and cook for about 10 minutes until they are half cooked.

2 Combine the crème fraîche with the stock, garlic and the chipotle salsa.

3 Arrange half the potatoes in a casserole dish. Pour half the crème fraîche sauce over the potatoes and cover with the goat's cheese. Top with the remaining potatoes and the sauce.

4 Sprinkle with the grated mozzarella or Cheddar cheese, then with either the grated Parmesan or pecorino.

5 Bake in a preheated oven at 180°C/350°F/Gas Mark 4 until the potatoes are tender and the cheese topping is lightly golden and crisped in places. Serve at once.

2

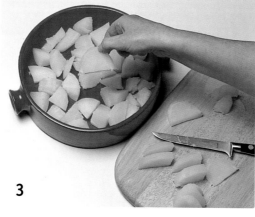

3

4

Main Meals

Packed with an amazing collection of international foods, this section allows you to treat yourself, or amaze your guests, with culinary delights from a range of continents. From the popular Mexican Enchiladas to the sophisticated Italian Ossobuco with Saffron Risotto, explore the tastiest and most popular dishes from around the world.

Tuna & Mushroom Ragout

INGREDIENTS

Serves 4

225 g/8 oz basmati and wild rice
50 g/2 oz butter
1 tbsp olive oil
1 large onion, peeled and
  finely chopped
1 garlic clove, peeled and crushed
300 g/11 oz baby button mushrooms,
  wiped and halved
2 tbsp plain flour
400 g can chopped tomatoes
1 tbsp freshly chopped parsley
dash of Worcestershire sauce
400 g can tuna in oil, drained
salt and freshly ground black pepper
4 tbsp Parmesan cheese, grated
1 tbsp freshly shredded basil

To serve:
green salad
garlic bread

TASTY TIP
If you have problems finding fresh basil, buy chopped tomatoes that have basil already added to them, or use extra freshly chopped parsley instead.

1　Cook the basmati and wild rice in a saucepan of boiling salted water for 20 minutes, then drain and return to the pan. Stir in half of the butter, cover the pan and leave to stand for 2 minutes until all of the butter has melted.

2　Heat the oil and the remaining butter in a frying pan and cook the onion for 1–2 minutes until soft. Add the garlic and mushrooms and continue to cook for a further 3 minutes.

3　Stir in the flour and cook for 1 minute, then add the tomatoes and bring the sauce to the boil. Add the parsley, Worcestershire sauce and tuna and simmer gently for 3 minutes. Season to taste with salt and freshly ground pepper.

4　Stir the rice well, then spoon onto 4 serving plates and top with the tuna and mushroom mixture. Sprinkle with a spoonful of grated Parmesan cheese and some shredded basil for each portion and serve immediately with a green salad and chunks of garlic bread.

Potato Boulangere with Sea Bass

INGREDIENTS

Serves 4

450 g/1 lb potatoes, peeled and
  thinly sliced
1 large onion, peeled and thinly sliced
salt and freshly ground black pepper
300 ml/½ pint fish
  or vegetable stock
75 g/3 oz butter or margarine
350 g/12 oz sea bass fillets
sprigs of fresh flat-leaf parsley,
  to garnish

1 Preheat the oven to 200°C/400°F/Gas Mark 6. Lightly grease a shallow 1.4 litre/2½ pint baking dish with oil or butter. Layer the potato slices and onions alternately in the prepared dish, seasoning each layer with salt and pepper.

2 Pour the stock over the top, then cut 50 g/2 oz of the butter or margarine into small pieces and dot over the top layer. Bake in the preheated oven for 50–60 minutes. Do not cover the dish at this stage.

3 Lightly rinse the sea bass fillets and pat dry on absorbent kitchen paper. Cook in a griddle, or heat the remaining butter or margarine in a frying pan and shallow fry the fish fillets for 3–4 minutes per side, flesh-side first. Remove from the pan with a slotted spatula and drain on absorbent kitchen paper.

4 Remove the partly cooked potato and onion mixture from the oven and place the fish on the top. Cover with tinfoil and return to the oven for 10 minutes until heated through. Garnish with sprigs of parsley and serve immediately.

FOOD FACT

Sea bass, also known as sea perch, is a large round fish which grows up to 1 m/3⅓ ft long, and may weigh up to 9 kg/20 lb. In appearance, it is similar to a salmon, but a much darker grey colour. Cook it gently and handle it with care, as the flesh is soft and delicate.

1

2

3

Jamaican Jerk Pork with Rice & Beans

INGREDIENTS

Serves 4

175 g/6 oz dried red kidney beans,
  soaked overnight
2 onions, peeled and chopped
2 garlic cloves, peeled and crushed
4 tbsp lime juice
2 tbsp each dark molasses, soy sauce
  and chopped fresh root ginger
2 jalapeño chillies, deseeded
  and chopped
½ tsp ground cinnamon
¼ tsp each ground allspice,
  ground nutmeg
4 pork loin chops, on the bone

For the rice:

1 tbsp vegetable oil
1 onion, peeled and finely chopped
1 celery stalk, trimmed and
  finely sliced
3 garlic cloves, peeled and crushed
2 bay leaves
225 g/8 oz long-grain white rice
475 ml/18 fl oz chicken or ham stock
sprigs of fresh flat-leaf parsley,
  to garnish

1 To make the jerk pork marinade, purée the onions, garlic, lime juice, molasses, soy sauce, ginger, chillies, cinnamon, allspice and nutmeg together in a food processor until smooth. Put the pork chops into a plastic or non-reactive dish and pour over the marinade, turning the chops to coat. Marinate in the refrigerator for at least 1 hour or overnight.

2 Drain the beans and place in a large saucepan with about 2 litres/3½ pints cold water. Bring to the boil and boil rapidly for 10 minutes. Reduce the heat, cover and simmer gently, for 1 hour until tender, adding more water, if necessary. When cooked, drain well and mash roughly.

3 Heat the oil for the rice in a saucepan with a tight-fitting lid and add the onion, celery and garlic. Cook gently for 5 minutes until softened. Add the bay leaves, rice and stock and stir. Bring to the boil, cover and cook very gently for 10 minutes. Add the beans and stir well again. Cook for a further 5 minutes, then remove from the heat.

4 Heat a griddle pan until almost smoking. Remove the pork chops from the marinade, scraping off any surplus and add to the hot pan. Cook for 5–8 minutes on each side, or until cooked. Garnish with the parsley and serve immediately with the rice.

3

1

1

Pork Goulash & Rice

INGREDIENTS

Serves 4

700 g/1½ lb boneless pork
rib chops
1 tbsp olive oil
2 onions, peeled and
  roughly chopped
1 red pepper, deseeded and
  sliced thinly
1 garlic clove, peeled and crushed
1 tbsp plain flour
1 rounded tbsp paprika
400 g can chopped tomatoes
salt and freshly ground black pepper
250 g/9 oz long-grain white rice
450 ml/¾ pint chicken stock
sprigs of fresh flat-leaf parsley,
  to garnish
150 ml/¼ pint soured cream,
  to serve

FOOD FACT

Paprika is the ground red powder from the dried pepper *Capsicum annum* and is a vital ingredient of goulash, giving it a distinctive colour and taste.

1   Preheat the oven to 140°C/275°F/Gas Mark 1. Cut the pork into large cubes, about 4 cm/1½ inches square. Heat the oil in a large flameproof casserole and brown the pork in batches over a high heat, transferring the cubes to a plate as they brown.

2   Over a medium heat, add the onions and pepper and cook for about 5 minutes, stirring regularly, until they begin to brown. Add the garlic and return the meat to the casserole along with any juices on the plate. Sprinkle in the flour and paprika and stir well to soak up the oil and juices.

3   Add the tomatoes and season to taste with salt and pepper. Bring slowly to the boil, cover with a tight-fitting lid and cook in the preheated oven for 1½ hours.

4   Meanwhile, rinse the rice in several changes of water until the water remains relatively clear. Drain well and put into a saucepan with the chicken stock or water and a little salt. Cover tightly and bring to the boil. Turn the heat down as low as possible and cook for 10 minutes without removing the lid. After 10 minutes, remove from the heat and leave for a further 10 minutes, without removing the lid. Fluff with a fork.

5   When the meat is tender, stir in the soured cream lightly to create a marbled effect, or serve separately. Garnish with parsley and serve immediately with the rice.

1

2

5

Nasi Goreng

INGREDIENTS

Serves 4

7 large shallots, peeled
1 red chilli, deseeded and
  roughly chopped
2 garlic cloves, peeled and
  roughly chopped
4 tbsp sunflower oil
2 tsp each tomato purée and
  Indonesian sweet soy sauce
  (katjap manis)
225 g/8 oz long-grain white rice
125 g/4 oz French beans, trimmed
3 medium eggs, beaten
pinch of sugar
salt and freshly ground black pepper
225 g/8 oz cooked ham, shredded
225 g/8 oz cooked peeled prawns,
  thawed if frozen
6 spring onions, trimmed and
  thinly sliced
1 tbsp light soy sauce
3 tbsp freshly chopped coriander

1. Roughly chop 1 of the shallots and place with the red chilli, garlic, 1 tablespoon of the oil, tomato purée and sweet soy sauce in a food processor and blend until smooth, then reserve. Boil the rice in plenty of salted water for 6–7 minutes until tender, adding the French beans after 4 minutes. Drain well and leave to cool.

2. Beat the eggs with the sugar and a little salt and pepper. Heat a little of the oil in a small non-stick frying pan and add about one-third of the egg mixture. Swirl to coat the base of the pan thinly and cook for about 1 minute until golden. Flip and cook the other side briefly before removing from the pan. Roll the omelette and slice thinly into strips. Repeat with the remaining egg to make 3 omelettes.

3. Thinly slice the remaining shallots then heat a further 2 tablespoons of the oil in a clean frying pan. Add the shallots to the pan and cook for 8–10 minutes over a medium heat until golden and crisp. Drain on absorbent kitchen paper and reserve.

4. Add the remaining 1 tablespoon of oil to a large wok or frying pan and fry the chilli paste over a medium heat for 1 minute. Add the cooked rice and beans and stir-fry for 2 minutes. Add the ham and prawns and continue stir-frying for a further 1–2 minutes. Add the omelette slices, half the fried shallots, the spring onions, soy sauce and chopped coriander. Stir-fry for a further minute until heated through. Spoon onto serving plates and garnish with the remaining crispy shallots. Serve immediately.

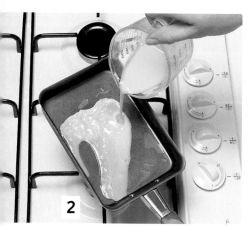

Beef Teriyaki with Green & Black Rice

INGREDIENTS

Serves 4

3 tbsp sake (Japanese rice wine)

3 tbsp dry sherry

3 tbsp dark soy sauce

1½ tbsp soft brown sugar

4 sirloin steaks, each weighing 175 g/
  6 oz, trimmed

350 g/12 oz long-grain and wild rice

2.5 cm/1 inch piece fresh root ginger

225 g/8 oz mangetout

salt

6 spring onions, trimmed and cut
  into fine strips

1. In a small saucepan, gently heat the sake, dry sherry, dark soy sauce and sugar until the sugar has dissolved. Increase the heat and bring to the boil. Remove from the heat and leave until cold. Lightly wipe the steaks, place in a shallow dish and pour the sake mixture over. Cover loosely and leave to marinate in the refrigerator for at least 1 hour, spooning the marinade over the steaks occasionally.

2. Cook the rice with the piece of root ginger, according to the packet instructions. Drain well, then remove and discard the piece of ginger.

3. Slice the mangetout thinly lengthways into fine shreds. Plunge into a saucepan of boiling salted water, return the water to the boil and drain immediately. Stir the drained mangetout and spring onions into the hot rice.

4. Meanwhile, heat a griddle pan until almost smoking. Remove the steaks from the marinade and cook on the hot grill pan for 3–4 minutes each side, depending on the thickness.

5. Place the remaining marinade in a saucepan and bring to the boil. Simmer rapidly for 2 minutes and remove from the heat. When the steaks are cooked to personal preference, leave to rest for 2–3 minutes, then slice thinly and serve with the rice and the hot marinade.

FOOD FACT

Before 1867, meat was prohibited in Japan in the belief that it would prevent aggression. The Japanese still eat a relatively small amount of meat and tend to use quick-cook tender cuts in dishes.

1

2

3

Spicy Chicken Skewers with Mango Tabbouleh

INGREDIENTS

Serves 4

400 g/14 oz chicken breast fillet
200 ml/7 fl oz natural low-fat yogurt
1 garlic clove, peeled and crushed
1 small red chilli, deseeded and
  finely chopped
½ tsp ground turmeric
finely grated rind and juice
  of ½ lemon
sprigs of fresh mint, to garnish

For the mango tabbouleh:

175 g/6 oz bulghur wheat
1 tsp olive oil
juice of ½ lemon
½ red onion, finely chopped
1 ripe mango, halved, stoned, peeled
  and chopped
¼ cucumber, finely diced
2 tbsp freshly chopped parsley
2 tbsp freshly shredded mint
salt and finely ground black pepper

1   If using wooden skewers, pre-soak them in cold water for at least 30 minutes. (This stops them from burning during grilling.)

2   Cut the chicken into 5 x 1 cm/2 x ½ inch strips and place in a shallow dish.

3   Mix together the yogurt, garlic, chilli, turmeric, lemon rind and juice. Pour over the chicken and toss to coat. Cover and leave to marinate in the refrigerator for up to 8 hours.

4   To make the tabbouleh, put the bulghur wheat in a bowl. Pour over enough boiling water to cover. Put a plate over the bowl. Leave to soak for 20 minutes.

5   Whisk together the oil and lemon juice in a bowl. Add the red onion and leave to marinade for 10 minutes.

6   Drain the bulghur wheat and squeeze out any excess moisture in a clean tea towel. Add to the red onion with the mango, cucumber, herbs and season to taste with salt and pepper. Toss together.

7   Thread the chicken strips on to 8 wooden or metal skewers. Cook under a hot grill for 8 minutes. Turn and brush with the marinade, until the chicken is lightly browned and cooked through.

8   Spoon the tabbouleh on to individual plates. Arrange the chicken skewers on top and garnish with the sprigs of mint. Serve warm or cold.

3

4

6

Mexican Chicken

INGREDIENTS

Serves 4

1.4 kg/3 lb oven-ready
  chicken, jointed
3 tbsp plain flour
$\frac{1}{2}$ tsp ground paprika pepper
salt and freshly ground black pepper
2 tsp sunflower oil
1 small onion, peeled and chopped
1 red chilli, deseeded and
  finely chopped
$\frac{1}{2}$ tsp ground cumin
$\frac{1}{2}$ tsp dried oregano
300 ml/$\frac{1}{2}$ pint chicken
  or vegetable stock
1 green pepper, deseeded and sliced
2 tsp cocoa powder
1 tbsp lime juice
2 tsp clear honey
3 tbsp 0%-fat Greek yogurt

To garnish:
sliced limes
red chilli slices
sprig of fresh oregano

To serve:
freshly cooked rice
fresh green salad leaves

1 Using a knife, remove the skin from the chicken joints.

2 In a shallow dish, mix together the flour, paprika, salt and pepper. Coat the chicken on both sides with flour and shake off any excess if necessary.

3 Heat the oil in a large non-stick frying pan. Add the chicken and brown on both sides. Transfer to a plate and reserve.

4 Add the onion and red chilli to the pan and gently cook for 5 minutes, or until the onion is soft. Stir occasionally.

5 Stir in the cumin and oregano and cook for a further minute. Pour in the stock and bring to the boil.

6 Return the chicken to the pan, cover and cook for 40 minutes. Add the green pepper and cook for 10 minutes, until the chicken is cooked. Remove the chicken and pepper with a slotted spoon and keep warm in a serving dish.

7 Blend the cocoa powder with 1 tablespoon of warm water. Stir into the sauce, then boil rapidly until the sauce has thickened and reduced by about one third. Stir in the lime juice, honey and yogurt.

8 Pour the sauce over the chicken and pepper and garnish with the lime slices, chilli and oregano. Serve immediately with the freshly cooked rice and green salad.

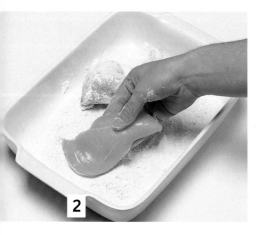

New Orleans Jambalaya

INGREDIENTS

Serves 6–8

For the seasoning mix:

2 dried bay leaves

1 tsp salt

2 tsp cayenne pepper, or to taste

2 tsp dried oregano

1 tsp each ground white and black
   pepper, or to taste

3 tbsp vegetable oil

125 g/4 oz ham

225 g/8 oz smoked pork sausage,
   cut into chunks

2 large onions, peeled and chopped

4 celery stalks, trimmed and chopped

2 green peppers, deseeded
   and chopped

2 garlic cloves, peeled and
   finely chopped

350 g/12 oz raw chicken, diced

400 g can chopped tomatoes

600 ml/1 pint fish stock

400 g/14 oz long-grain white rice

4 spring onions, trimmed and
   coarsely chopped

275 g/10 oz raw prawns, peeled

250 g/9 oz white crab meat

1 Mix all the seasoning ingredients together in a small bowl and reserve.

2 Heat 2 tablespoons of the oil in a large flameproof casserole over a medium heat. Add the ham and sausage and cook, stirring often, for 7–8 minutes until golden. Remove from the pan and reserve.

3 Add the onions, celery and peppers to the casserole and cook for about 4 minutes, or until softened, stirring occasionally. Stir in the garlic, then using a slotted spoon, transfer all the vegetables to a plate and reserve with the sausage.

4 Add the chicken pieces to the casserole and cook for about 4 minutes, or until beginning to colour, turning once. Stir in the seasoning mix and turn the pieces to coat well. Return the sausage and vegetables to the casserole and stir well. Add the chopped tomatoes, with their juice, and the stock and bring to the boil.

5 Stir in the rice and reduce the heat to low. Cover and simmer for 12 minutes. Uncover, stir in the spring onions and prawns and cook, covered, for a further 4 minutes. Add the crab and gently stir in. Cook for 2–3 minutes, or until the rice is tender. Remove from the heat, cover and leave to stand for 5 minutes before serving.

2

4

5

Spiced Couscous & Vegetables

INGREDIENTS

Serves 4

1 tbsp olive oil

1 large shallot, peeled and
finely chopped

1 garlic clove, peeled and
finely chopped

1 small red pepper, deseeded and cut
into strips

1 small yellow pepper, deseeded and
cut into strips

1 small aubergine, diced

1 tsp each turmeric, ground cumin,
ground cinnamon and paprika

2 tsp ground coriander

large pinch saffron strands

2 tomatoes, peeled, deseeded
and diced

2 tbsp lemon juice

225 g/8 oz couscous

225 ml/8 fl oz vegetable stock

2 tbsp raisins

2 tbsp whole almonds

2 tbsp freshly chopped parsley

2 tbsp freshly chopped coriander

salt and freshly ground black pepper

1 Heat the oil in a large frying pan and add the shallot and garlic and cook for 2–3 minutes until softened. Add the peppers and aubergine and reduce the heat.

2 Cook for 8–10 minutes until the vegetables are tender, adding a little water if necessary.

3 Test a piece of aubergine to ensure it is cooked through. Add all the spices and cook for a further minute, stirring.

4 Increase the heat and add the tomatoes and lemon juice. Cook for 2–3 minutes until the tomatoes have started to break down. Remove from the heat and leave to cool slightly.

5 Meanwhile, put the couscous into a large bowl. Bring the stock to the boil in a saucepan, then pour over the couscous. Stir well and cover with a clean tea towel.

6 Leave to stand for 7–8 minutes until all the stock is absorbed and the couscous is tender.

7 Uncover the couscous and fluff with a fork. Stir in the vegetable and spice mixture along with the raisins, almonds, parsley and coriander. Season to taste with salt and pepper and serve.

3

5

7

Black Bean Chilli with Avocado Salsa

INGREDIENTS

Serves 4

250 g/9 oz black beans

2 tbsp olive oil

1 large onion, peeled and
finely chopped

1 red pepper, deseeded and diced

2 garlic cloves, peeled and
finely chopped

1 red chilli, deseeded and
finely chopped

2 tsp chilli powder

1 tsp ground cumin

2 tsp ground coriander

400 g can chopped tomatoes

450 ml/³/₄ pint vegetable stock

1 small ripe avocado, diced

½ small red onion, peeled and
finely chopped

2 tbsp freshly chopped coriander

juice of 1 lime

1 small tomato, peeled, deseeded
and diced

salt and freshly ground black pepper

25 g/1 oz dark chocolate

To garnish:

half-fat crème fraîche

lime slices

sprigs of coriander

1 Soak the beans overnight. Drain the beans and place in a large saucepan with at least twice their volume of fresh water.

2 Bring slowly to the boil, skimming off any froth that rises to the surface. Boil rapidly for 10 minutes, then reduce the heat and simmer for about 45 minutes, adding more water if necessary. Drain and reserve.

3 Heat the oil in a large saucepan and add the onion and pepper. Cook for 3–4 minutes until softened. Add the garlic and chilli. Cook for 5 minutes, or until the onion and pepper have softened. Add the chilli powder, cumin and coriander and cook for 30 seconds. Add the beans along with the tomatoes and stock.

4 Bring to the boil and simmer uncovered for 40–45 minutes until the beans and vegetables are tender and the sauce has reduced.

5 Mix together the avocado, onion, fresh coriander, lime juice and tomato. Season with salt and pepper and set aside. Remove the chilli from the heat. Break the chocolate into pieces. Sprinkle over the chilli. Leave for 2 minutes. Stir well. Garnish with crème fraîche, lime and coriander. Serve with the avocado salsa.

Chunky Vegetable & Fennel Goulash with Dumplings

INGREDIENTS

Serves 4

2 fennel bulbs, weighing
  about 450 g/1 lb
2 tbsp sunflower oil
1 large onion, peeled and sliced
1½ tbsp paprika
1 tbsp plain flour
300 ml/½ pint vegetable stock
400 g can chopped tomatoes
450 g/1 lb potatoes, peeled and cut
  into 2.5 cm/1 inch chunks
125 g/4 oz small button mushrooms
salt and freshly ground black pepper

For the dumplings:

1 tbsp sunflower oil
1 small onion, peeled and
  finely chopped
1 medium egg
3 tbsp milk
3 tbsp freshly chopped parsley
125 g/4 oz fresh white breadcrumbs

TASTY TIP

Soured cream or crème fraîche
would be delicious if spooned on
top of the goulash.

1. Cut the fennel bulbs in half widthways. Thickly slice the stalks and cut the bulbs into 8 wedges. Heat the oil in a large saucepan or flameproof casserole. Add the onion and fennel and cook gently for 10 minutes until soft. Stir in the paprika and flour.

2. Remove from the heat and gradually stir in the stock. Add the chopped tomatoes, potatoes and mushrooms. Season to taste with salt and pepper. Bring to the boil, reduce the heat and simmer for 20 minutes.

3. Meanwhile, make the dumplings. Heat the oil in a frying pan and gently cook the onion for 10 minutes, until soft. Leave to cool for a few minutes.

4. In a bowl, beat the egg and milk together, then add the onion, parsley, breadcrumbs, and season to taste. With damp hands form the breadcrumb mixture into 12 round dumplings each about the size of a walnut.

5. Arrange the dumplings on top of the goulash. Cover and cook for a further 15 minutes, until the dumplings are cooked and the vegetables are tender. Serve immediately.

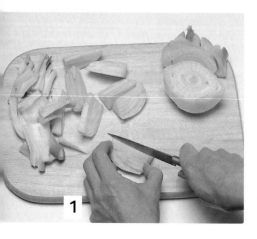
1

2

4

Lamb & Potato Moussaka

INGREDIENTS

Serves 4

700 g/1½ lb cooked roast lamb

700 g/1½ lb potatoes, peeled

125 g/4 oz butter

1 large onion, peeled and chopped

2–4 garlic cloves, peeled and crushed

3 tbsp tomato purée

1 tbsp freshly chopped parsley

salt and freshly ground black pepper

3–4 tbsp olive oil

2 medium aubergines,
  trimmed and sliced

4 medium tomatoes, sliced

2 medium eggs

300 ml/½ pint Greek yogurt

2–3 tbsp Parmesan cheese, grated

TASTY TIP

It is worth salting aubergines to ensure that any bitterness is removed. Layer the slices in a colander, sprinkling a little salt between the layers. Leave for 20 minutes, then rinse under cold running water and pat dry on absorbent kitchen paper.

1 Preheat the oven to 200°C/400°F/Gas Mark 6, about 15 minutes before required. Trim the lamb, discarding any fat then cut into fine dice and reserve. Thinly slice the potatoes and rinse thoroughly in cold water, then pat dry with a clean tea towel.

2 Melt 50 g/2 oz of the butter in a frying pan and fry the potatoes, in batches, until crisp and golden. Using a slotted spoon, remove from the pan and reserve. Use a third of the potatoes to line the base of an ovenproof dish.

3 Add the onion and garlic to the butter remaining in the pan and cook for 5 minutes. Add the lamb and fry for 1 minute. Blend the tomato purée with 3 tablespoons of water and stir into the pan with the parsley and salt and pepper. Spoon over the layer of potatoes, then top with the remaining potato slices.

4 Heat the oil and the remaining butter in the pan and brown the aubergine slices for 5–6 minutes. Arrange the tomatoes on top of the potatoes, then the aubergines on top of the tomatoes. Beat the eggs with the yogurt and Parmesan cheese and pour over the aubergine and tomatoes. Bake in the preheated oven for 25 minutes, or until golden and piping hot. Serve.

Broccoli Enchiladas in Mild Chilli Salsa

INGREDIENTS

Serves 4

450 g/1 lb broccoli florets

225 g/8 oz ricotta cheese

1 garlic clove, chopped

½ tsp ground cumin

175–200 g/6–8 oz Cheddar
   cheese, grated

6–8 tbsp freshly grated
   Parmesan cheese

1 egg, lightly beaten

4–6 flour tortillas

vegetable oil, for greasing

1 quantity Mild Red Chilli Sauce

225 ml/8 fl oz chicken or
   vegetable stock

½ onion, finely chopped

3–4 tbsp chopped fresh coriander

3 ripe tomatoes, diced

salt and pepper

hot salsa, to serve

1 Bring a pan of salted water to the boil, add the broccoli, bring back to the boil and blanch for 1 minute. Drain, refresh under cold running water, then drain again. Cut off the stems, peel and chop. Dice the heads.

2 Mix the broccoli with the ricotta cheese, garlic, cumin, half the Cheddar and Parmesan in a bowl. Mix in the egg and season with salt and pepper.

3 Heat the tortillas in a lightly greased non-stick frying pan, then wrap in kitchen foil. Fill the tortillas with the broccoli mixture, rolling them up.

4 Arrange the tortilla rolls in an ovenproof dish, then pour the mild chilli sauce over the top. Pour over the stock.

5 Top with the remaining Cheddar and Parmesan cheeses and bake in a preheated oven at 190°C/375°F/Gas Mark 5 for about 30 minutes. Serve sprinkled with the onion, fresh coriander and tomatoes. Serve with a hot salsa.

2

3

4

Huevos Tapatios

INGREDIENTS

Serves 4

4 corn tortillas

1 avocado

lime or lemon juice, for tossing

175 g/6 oz chorizo sausage,
  sliced or diced

2 tbsp butter or water, for cooking

4 eggs

4 tbsp feta or Wensleydale
  cheese, crumbled

salsa of your choice

1 tbsp chopped fresh coriander

1 tbsp finely chopped spring onions

1   Heat the tortillas in an ungreased non-stick frying pan, sprinkling them with a few drops of water as they heat. wWap the tortillas in a clean tea towel as you work to keep them warm. Alternatively, heat through in a stack in the pan, alternating the top and bottom tortillas so that they warm evenly. Wrap to keep warm.

2   Cut the avocado in half around the stone. Twist apart, then remove the stone with a knife. Carefully peel off the skin, dice the flesh and toss in lime or lemon juice to prevent discoloration.

3   Brown the chorizo sausage in a pan, then arrange on each warmed tortilla. Keep warm.

4   Meanwhile, heat the butter or water in the non-stick frying pan, break in an egg and cook until the white is set but the yolk still soft. Remove from the pan and place on top of one tortilla. Keep warm.

5   Cook the remaining eggs in the same way, adding to the tortillas.

6   Arrange the avocado, cheese and a spoonful of salsa on each tortilla. Add the fresh coriander and spring onions and serve.

3

4

6

Lime-baked Fish

INGREDIENTS

Serves 4

1 kg/2 lb 4 oz white fish fillets, such
   as bass, plaice or cod
1 lime, halved
3 tbsp extra-virgin olive oil
1 large onion, finely chopped
3 garlic cloves, finely chopped
2–3 pickled jalapeño
   chillies, chopped
6–8 tbsp chopped fresh coriander
salt and pepper
lemon and lime wedges, to serve

1 Place the fish fillets in a bowl and sprinkle with salt and pepper. Squeeze the juice from the lime over the fish.

2 Heat the olive oil in a frying pan. Add the onion and garlic and fry for about 2 minutes, stirring frequently, until softened. Remove from the heat.

3 Place a third of the onion mixture and a little of the chillies and coriander in the bottom of a shallow baking dish or roasting tin. Arrange the fish on top. Top with the remaining onion mixture, chillies and coriander.

4 Bake in a preheated oven at 180°C/350°F/Gas Mark 4 for about 15–20 minutes or until the fish has become slightly opaque and firm to the touch. Serve at once, with lemon and lime wedges for squeezing over the fish.

TASTY TIP
Add sliced flavourful fresh tomatoes, or canned chopped tomatoes, to the onion mixture at the end of Step 2.

1

3

3

Duck with Mole Sauce & Pineapple

INGREDIENTS

Serves 4

1 duck, cut into 4 pieces
juice of 2 limes
120 ml/ 4 fl oz pineapple juice
5–8 garlic cloves, sliced or chopped
a few shakes of mild red chilli
   powder, such as ancho
2 tbsp sugar
salt
½ pineapple, peeled and cut
   into slices
450 ml/16 fl oz/2 cups mole sauce
salt
fresh chilli strips, to garnish

1 Combine the duck with the lime juice, pineapple juice, garlic, chilli powder, salt and half the sugar. Leave to marinate for at least 2 hours, preferably overnight in the refrigerator.

2 Remove the duck from the marinade and pat dry with paper towels. Arrange the dark meat in a roasting tin (pan) and roast in a preheated oven at 160°C/325°F/Gas Mark 3 for about 20 minutes. Pour off the fat as it renders from the duck.

3 Add the breast pieces and continue to roast slowly for about 20 more minutes. Pour off the fat. Increase the temperature to 200–220°C/400–425°F/Gas Mark 6–7 for 5–10 minutes or until crisp and brown the duck.

4 Warm the mole sauce with enough water to prevent it from sticking and burning. Set aside and keep warm.

5 Sprinkle the pineapple with the remaining sugar and grill on both sides until the pineapple is lightly browned.

6 Serve the duck portions accompanied by the pineapple slices and topped with the mole sauce. Garnish with chilli and serve.

2

3

5

Lentils Simmered with Fruit

INGREDIENTS

Serves 4

125 g/4½ oz brown or green lentils

about 1 litre/1¾ pints water

2 tbsp vegetable oil

3 small to medium onions, chopped

4 garlic cloves, coarsely chopped

1 large tart apple, roughly chopped

about ¼ ripe pineapple, skin removed
  and roughly chopped

2 tomatoes, deseeded and diced

1 almost ripe banana, cut into
  bite-sized pieces

salt

cayenne pepper, to taste

fresh parsley sprig, to garnish

1 Combine the lentils with the water in a pan, then bring to the boil. Reduce the heat and simmer over a low heat for about 40 minutes until the lentils are tender. Do not let them get mushy.

2 Meanwhile, heat the oil in a frying pan and fry the onions and garlic until lightly browned and softened. Add the apple and continue to cook until golden. Add the pineapple, heat through, stirring, then add the tomatoes. Cook over a medium heat until thickened, stirring occasionally.

3 Drain the lentils, reserving 120 ml/4 fl oz of the cooking liquid. Add the drained lentils to the sauce, stirring in the reserved liquid if necessary. Heat through for a minute to mingle the flavours.

4 Add the banana to the pan, then season with salt and cayenne pepper. Serve garnished with parsley.

TASTY TIP

Instead of lentils, prepare this dish using cooked pinto or cranberry beans.

Mussels Cooked with Lager

INGREDIENTS

Serves 4

1.5 kg/3 lb 5 oz live mussels
450 ml/16 fl oz lager
2 onions, chopped
5 garlic cloves, chopped coarsely
1 fresh green chilli, such as
   jalapeño or serrano,
   deseeded and thinly sliced
175 g/6 oz fresh tomatoes, diced,
   or canned chopped
2–3 tbsp chopped fresh coriander

1 Scrub the mussels under cold running water to remove any mud. Using a sharp knife, cut away the feathery 'beards' from the shells. Discard any open mussels that do not shut when tapped sharply with a knife. Rinse again in cold water.

2 Place the lager, onions, garlic, chilli and tomatoes in a heavy-based pan. Bring to the boil.

3 Add the mussels and cook, covered, over a medium-high heat for about 10 minutes until the shells open. Discard any mussels that do not open.

4 Ladle into individual bowls and serve sprinkled with fresh coriander.

TASTY TIP

Add the kernels from 2 ears of corn to the lager mixture in Step 2. A pinch of sugar might be needed to bring out the sweetness of the corn.

1

2

3

Huevos Oazaquena

INGREDIENTS

Serves 4

1 kg/2 lb 4 oz ripe tomatoes
about 12 small button onions, halved
8 garlic cloves, whole and unpeeled
2 fresh mild green chillies
pinch of ground cumin
pinch of dried oregano,
pinch of sugar, if needed
2–3 tsp vegetable oil
8 eggs, lightly beaten
1–2 tbsp tomato purée
salt and pepper
1–2 tbsp chopped fresh coriander,
  to garnish

1 Heat an ungreased heavy-based frying pan, add the tomatoes and char lightly, turning them once or twice. Allow to cool.

2 Meanwhile lightly char the onions, garlic and chillies in the pan. Allow to cool slightly.

3 Cut the cooled tomatoes into pieces and place in a blender or food processor, with their charred skins. Remove the stems and seeds from the chillies, then peel and chop. Remove the skins from the garlic, then chop. Roughly chop the onions. Add the chillies, garlic and onions to the tomatoes.

4 Process to make a rough purée, then add the cumin and oregano. Season with salt and pepper to taste, and add sugar if needed.

5 Heat the oil in a non-stick frying pan, add a ladleful of egg and cook to make a thin omelette. Continue to make omelettes, stacking them on a plate as they are cooked. Slice into noodle-like ribbons.

6 Bring the sauce to the boil, adjust the seasoning, adding tomato purée to taste. Add the omelette strips, warm through and serve at once, garnished with a sprinkling of fresh coriander.

Chicken Thighs with Yucatecan–flavoured Vinegar Sauce

INGREDIENTS

Serves 4

8 small boned chicken thighs
chicken stock
15–20 garlic cloves, unpeeled
1 tsp cumin seeds, lightly toasted
1 tsp coarsely ground black pepper
$\frac{1}{2}$ tsp ground cloves
2 tsp crumbled dried oregano or
  $\frac{1}{2}$ tsp crushed or powdered
  bay leaves
about $\frac{1}{2}$ tsp salt
1 tbsp lime juice
1 tbsp flour, plus extra for dredging
  the chicken
3–4 onions, thinly sliced
2 fresh chillies, preferably mildish
  yellow ones, such as Mexican
  Guero or similar Turkish or Greek
  chillies, deseeded and sliced
120 ml/4 fl oz vegetable oil
100 ml/3$\frac{1}{2}$ fl oz cider or
  sherry vinegar

1 Place the chicken in a pan with enough stock to cover. Bring to the boil, then reduce the heat and simmer for 5 minutes. Remove from the heat and allow the chicken to cool in the stock; the chicken will continue to cook as it cools in the hot stock.

2 Meanwhile, roast the garlic cloves in an ungreased heavy-based non-stick frying pan until they are lightly browned on all sides and tender inside. Remove from the heat. When cool enough to handle, squeeze the flesh from the skins and place in a bowl.

3 Grind the garlic with the pepper, cloves, oregano, salt, lime juice and three-quarters of the cumin seeds. Mix with the flour.

4 When the chicken is cool, remove from the stock and pat dry. Reserve the stock. Rub the chicken with about two-thirds of the garlic-spice paste and stand at room temperature for at least 30 minutes or up to overnight in the refrigerator.

5 Fry the onions and chillies in a tiny bit of the oil until golden brown and softened. Pour in the vinegar and remaining cumin seeds, cook for a few minutes, then add the reserved stock and remaining spice paste. Boil, stirring, for about 10 minutes until reduced in volume.

6 Dredge the chicken in flour. Heat the remaining oil in a heavy-based frying pan. Fry the chicken until lightly browned, then remove from the pan and serve immediately, each portion topped with the onion and vinegar sauce.

2

4

6

Traditional Provençale Daube

INGREDIENTS

Serves 4–6

700 g/1 lb 9 oz boneless lean stewing
beef, such as leg, cut into 5 cm/
2 inch pieces

400 ml/14 fl oz full-bodied dry
red wine

2 tbsp olive oil

4 large garlic cloves, crushed

4 shallots, thinly sliced

250 g/9 oz unsmoked lardons

5–6 tbsp plain flour

250 g/9 oz large chestnut
mushrooms, sliced

400 g/14 oz can chopped tomatoes

1 large bouquet garni of 1 bay leaf,
2 sprigs dried thyme and 2 sprigs
fresh parsley, tied in a 7.5 cm/3 inch
piece of celery

5 cm/2 inch strip dried orange
rind (optional)

450 ml/16 fl oz oz beef stock

50 g/1³/₄ oz can anchovy fillets in oil

2 tbsp capers in brine, drained

2 tbsp red wine vinegar

2 tbsp finely chopped fresh parsley

salt and pepper

1 Place the stewing beef in a non-metallic bowl with the wine, olive oil, half the garlic and the shallots. Cover and leave to marinate for at least 4 hours, stirring occasionally.

2 Meanwhile, place the lardons in a pan of water, bring to the boil and simmer for 10 minutes. Drain.

3 Place 4 tablespoons of the flour in a bowl and stir in about 2 tablespoons water to make a thick paste. Cover and set aside.

4 Strain the marinated beef, reserving the marinade. Pat the beef dry and toss in seasoned flour.

5 Arrange a layer of lardons, mushrooms and tomatoes in a large flameproof casserole dish, then add a layer of beef. Continue layering until all the ingredients are used, tucking in the bouquet garni and orange rind, if using.

6 Pour in the beef stock and reserved marinade. Spread the flour paste around the rim of the casserole dish. Press on the lid to make a tight seal (make more paste if necessary).

7 Cook in a preheated oven at 160°C/325°F/Gas Mark 3 for 2½ hours. Meanwhile, drain the anchovies, then mash with the capers and remaining garlic.

8 Remove the casserole dish, break the seal and stir in the mashed anchovies, vinegar and parsley. Re-cover and continue cooking for 1–1½ hours until the meat is tender. Adjust the seasoning and serve.

5

7

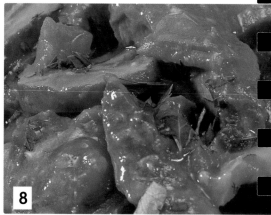

8

Sea Bass in Creamy Watercress & Prosciutto Sauce

INGREDIENTS

Serves 4

75 g/3 oz watercress
450 ml/³/₄ pint fish
  or chicken stock
150 ml/¹/₄ pint dry white wine
225 g/8 oz tagliatelle pasta
40 g/1¹/₂ oz butter
75 g/3 oz prosciutto ham
2 tbsp plain flour
300 ml/¹/₂ pint single cream
salt and freshly ground black pepper
olive oil, for spraying
4 x 175 g/6 oz sea bass fillets
fresh watercress, to garnish

1 Remove the leaves from the watercress stalks and reserve. Chop the stalks roughly and put in a large pan with the stock. Bring to the boil slowly, cover, and simmer for 20 minutes. Strain, and discard the stalks. Make the stock up to 300 ml/¹/₂ pint with the wine.

2 Bring a large saucepan of lightly salted water to the boil and cook the pasta for 8–10 minutes or until 'al dente'. Drain and reserve.

3 Melt the butter in a saucepan, and cook the prosciutto gently for 3 minutes. Remove with a slotted spoon. Stir the flour into the saucepan and cook on a medium heat for 2 minutes. Remove from the heat and gradually pour in the hot watercress stock, stirring continuously. Return to the heat and bring to the boil, stirring throughout. Simmer for 3 minutes, or until the sauce has thickened and is smooth. Purée the watercress leaves and cream in a food processor then add to the sauce with the prosciutto. Season to taste with salt and pepper, add the pasta, toss lightly and keep warm.

4 Meanwhile, spray a griddle pan lightly with olive oil, then heat until hot. When hot, cook the fillets for 3–4 minutes on each side, or until cooked. Arrange the sea bass on a bed of pasta and drizzle with a little sauce. Garnish with watercress and serve immediately.

HELPFUL HINT

Always wash watercress thoroughly before using, then either dry in a clean tea towel or a salad spinner to remove all the excess moisture.

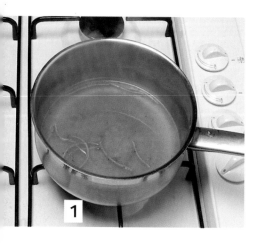

1

3

3

Spaghetti alle Vongole

INGREDIENTS

Serves 4

1.8 kg/4 lb small fresh clams
6 tbsp dry white wine
2 tbsp olive oil
1 small onion, peeled and
  finely chopped
2 garlic cloves, peeled and crushed
400 g/14 oz spaghetti
2 tbsp freshly chopped parsley
2 tbsp freshly chopped or torn basil
salt and freshly ground black pepper
oregano leaves, to garnish

HELPFUL HINT

Cook and eat clams within 24 hours of buying them. Steam them until the shells have just opened, as overcooking will toughen them.

1 Soak the clams in lightly salted cold water for 8 hours before required, changing the water once or twice. Scrub the clams, removing any that have broken shells or that remain open when tapped.

2 Place the prepared clams in a large saucepan and pour in the wine. Cover with a tight-fitting lid and cook over a medium heat for 5–6 minutes, shaking the pan occasionally, until the shells have opened.

3 Strain the clams and cooking juices through a sieve lined with muslin and reserve. Discard any clams that have remained unopened.

4 Heat the olive oil in a saucepan and fry the onion and garlic gently for 10 minutes, or until very soft.

5 Meanwhile, bring a large pan of lightly salted water to a rolling boil. Add the spaghetti and cook according to the packet instructions, or until 'al dente'.

6 Add the cooked clams to the onions and garlic and pour in the reserved cooking juices. Bring to the boil, then add the parsley and basil and season to taste with salt and black pepper.

7 Drain the spaghetti thoroughly. Return to the pan and add the clams with their sauce. Toss together gently, then tip into a large warmed serving bowl or into individual bowls. Serve immediately, sprinkled with oregano leaves.

2

3

6

Hot Salami & Vegetable Gratin

INGREDIENTS

Serves 4

350 g/12 oz carrots
175 g/6 oz fine green beans
250 g/9 oz asparagus tips
175 g/6 oz frozen peas
225 g/8 oz Italian salami
1 tbsp olive oil
1 tbsp freshly chopped mint
25 g/1 oz butter
150 g/5 oz baby spinach leaves
150 ml/¼ pint double cream
salt and freshly ground black pepper
1 small or ½ an olive ciabatta loaf
75 g/3 oz Parmesan cheese, grated
green salad, to serve

1 Preheat oven to 200°C/400°F/Gas Mark 6. Peel and slice the carrots, trim the beans and asparagus and reserve. Cook the carrots in a saucepan of lightly salted, boiling water for 5 minutes. Add the remaining vegetables, except the spinach, and cook for about a further 5 minutes, or until tender. Drain and place in an ovenproof dish.

2 Discard any skin from the outside of the salami, if necessary, then chop roughly. Heat the oil in a frying pan and fry the salami for 4–5 minutes, stirring occasionally, until golden. Using a slotted spoon, transfer the salami to the ovenproof dish and scatter over the mint.

3 Add the butter to the frying pan and cook the spinach for 1–2 minutes, or until just wilted. Stir in the double cream and season well with salt and pepper. Spoon the mixture over the vegetables.

4 Whizz the ciabatta loaf in a food processor to make breadcrumbs. Stir in the Parmesan cheese and sprinkle over the vegetables. Bake in the preheated oven for 20 minutes, until golden and heated through. Serve with a green salad.

TASTY TIP

Prepare this dish ahead up to the end of step 3 and refrigerate until ready to cook, then top with breadcrumbs and bake, adding about 5 minutes to the final cooking time.

1

2

4

Rabbit Italian

INGREDIENTS

Serves 4

450 g/1 lb diced rabbit, thawed
   if frozen
6 rashers streaky bacon
1 garlic clove, peeled
1 onion, peeled
1 carrot, peeled
1 celery stalk
25 g/1 oz butter
2 tbsp olive oil
400 g can chopped tomatoes
150 ml/¼ pint red wine
salt and freshly ground black pepper
125 g/4 oz mushrooms

To serve:
freshly cooked pasta
green salad

1 Trim the rabbit if necessary. Chop the bacon and reserve. Chop the garlic and onion and slice the carrot thinly, then trim the celery and chop.

2 Heat the butter and 1 tablespoon of the oil in a large saucepan and brown the rabbit for 5 minutes, stirring frequently, until sealed all over. Transfer the rabbit to a plate and reserve.

3 Add the garlic, bacon, celery, carrot and onion to the saucepan and cook for a further 5 minutes, stirring occasionally, until softened, then return the rabbit to the saucepan and pour over the tomatoes with their juice and the wine. Season to taste with salt and pepper. Bring to the boil, cover, reduce the heat and simmer for 45 minutes.

4 Meanwhile, wipe the mushrooms and if large, cut in half. Heat the remaining oil in a small frying pan and sauté the mushrooms for 2 minutes. Drain, then add to the rabbit and cook for 15 minutes, or until the rabbit is tender. Season to taste and serve immediately with freshly cooked pasta and a green salad.

HELPFUL HINT

If you prefer to buy a whole rabbit, have your butcher joint it for you into 8 pieces. The method and cooking time will remain the same.

Ossobuco with Saffron Risotto

INGREDIENTS

Serves 4

125 g/4 oz butter
2 tbsp olive oil
4 large pieces of shin of veal (often
  sold as ossobuco)
2 onions, peeled and
  roughly chopped
2 garlic cloves, peeled and
  finely chopped
300 ml/½ pint white wine
5 plum tomatoes, peeled
  and chopped
1 tbsp tomato purée
salt and freshly ground black pepper
2 tbsp freshly chopped parsley
grated rind of 1 small lemon
few strands of saffron, crushed
350 g/12 oz Arborio rice
1.3 litres/2¼ pints chicken
  stock, heated
50 g/2 oz Parmesan cheese, grated

1   Heat 50 g/2 oz butter with half the oil in a large saucepan and
    add the pieces of veal. Brown lightly on both sides, then transfer
    to a plate. Add half the onion and garlic and cook gently for about
    10 minutes until the onion is just golden.

2   Return the veal to the saucepan along with the white wine, tomatoes
    and tomato purée. Season lightly with salt and pepper, cover and
    bring to a gentle simmer. Cook very gently for 1 hour. Uncover and
    cook for a further 30 minutes until the meat is cooked and the
    sauce is reduced and thickened. Season to taste. Mix together the
    remaining garlic, parsley and lemon rind and reserve.

3   Meanwhile, slowly melt the remaining butter and oil in a large
    deep-sided frying pan. Add the remaining onion and cook gently
    for 5–7 minutes until just brown. Add the saffron and stir for a few
    seconds, then add the rice. Cook for a further minute until the rice
    is well coated in oil and butter.

4   Begin adding the stock a ladleful at a time, stirring well after each
    addition of stock and waiting until it is absorbed before adding the
    next. Continue in this way until all the stock is used. Remove from
    the heat and stir in the grated Parmesan cheese and seasoning.

5   Spoon a little of the saffron risotto onto each of 4 serving plates.
    Top with the ossobuco and sauce and sprinkle over the reserved
    garlic and parsley mixture. Serve immediately.

Chicken Basquaise

INGREDIENTS

Serves 4–6

1.4 kg/3 lb chicken, cut into 8 pieces

2 tbsp plain flour

salt and freshly ground black pepper

3 tbsp olive oil

1 large onion, peeled and sliced

2 red peppers, deseeded and cut into
thick strips

2 garlic cloves, peeled and crushed

150 g/5 oz spicy chorizo sausage cut
into 1 cm/½ inch pieces

200 g/7 oz long-grain white rice

450 ml/¾ pint chicken stock

1 tsp crushed dried chillies

½ tsp dried thyme

1 tbsp tomato purée

125 g/4 oz Spanish air-dried
ham, diced

12 black olives

2 tbsp freshly chopped parsley

1 Dry the chicken pieces well with absorbent kitchen paper. Put the flour in a polythene bag, season with salt and pepper and add the chicken pieces. Twist the bag to seal, then shake to coat the chicken pieces thoroughly.

2 Heat 2 tablespoons of the oil in a large heavy-based saucepan over a medium-high heat. Add the chicken pieces and cook for about 15 minutes, turning on all sides, until well browned. Using a slotted spoon, transfer to a plate.

3 Add the remaining olive oil to the saucepan, then add the onion and peppers. Reduce the heat to medium and cook, stirring frequently, until starting to colour and soften. Stir in the garlic and chorizo and continue to cook for a further 3 minutes. Add the rice and cook for about 2 minutes, stirring to coat with the oil, until the rice is translucent and golden.

4 Stir in the stock, crushed chillies, thyme, tomato purée and salt and pepper and bring to the boil. Return the chicken to the saucepan, pressing gently into the rice. Cover and cook over a very low heat for about 45 minutes until the chicken and rice are cooked and tender.

5 Gently stir in the ham, black olives and half the parsley. Cover and heat for a further 5 minutes. Sprinkle with the remaining parsley and serve immediately.

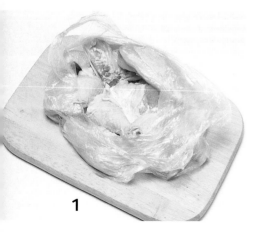

1

3

5

Persian Chicken Pilaf

INGREDIENTS

Serves 4–6

2–3 tbsp vegetable oil

700 g/1½ lb boneless skinless
   chicken pieces (breast and thighs),
   cut into 2.5 cm/1 inch pieces

2 medium onions, peeled and
   coarsely chopped

1 tsp ground cumin

200 g/7 oz long-grain white rice

1 tbsp tomato purée

1 tsp saffron strands

salt and freshly ground black pepper

100 ml/3½ fl oz pomegranate juice

900 ml/1½ pints chicken stock

125 g/4 oz ready-to-eat dried apricots
   or prunes, halved

2 tbsp raisins

2 tbsp freshly chopped mint
   or parsley

pomegranate seeds,
   to garnish (optional)

1 Heat the oil in a large heavy-based saucepan over a medium-high heat. Cook the chicken pieces, in batches, until lightly browned. Return all the browned chicken to the saucepan.

2 Add the onions to the saucepan, reduce the heat to medium and cook for 3–5 minutes, stirring frequently, until the onions begin to soften. Add the cumin and rice and stir to coat the rice. Cook for about 2 minutes until the rice is golden and translucent. Stir in the tomato purée and the saffron strands, then season to taste with salt and pepper.

3 Add the pomegranate juice and stock and bring to the boil, stirring once or twice. Add the apricots or prunes and raisins and stir gently. Reduce the heat to low and cook for 30 minutes until the chicken and rice are tender and the liquid is absorbed.

4 Turn into a shallow serving dish and sprinkle with the chopped mint or parsley. Serve immediately, garnished with pomegranate seeds, if using.

2

3

1

Pumpkin & Chickpea Curry

INGREDIENTS

Serves 4

1 tbsp vegetable oil

1 small onion, peeled and sliced

2 garlic cloves, peeled and
 finely chopped

2.5 cm/1 inch piece root ginger,
 peeled and grated

1 tsp ground coriander

½ tsp ground cumin

½ tsp ground turmeric

¼ tsp ground cinnamon

2 tomatoes, chopped

2 red bird's-eye chillies, deseeded
 and finely chopped

450 g/1 lb pumpkin or butternut
 squash flesh, cubed

1 tbsp hot curry paste

300 ml/½ pint vegetable stock

1 large firm banana

400 g can chickpeas, drained
 and rinsed

salt and freshly ground black pepper

1 tbsp freshly chopped coriander

coriander sprigs, to garnish

rice or naan bread, to serve

1 Heat 1 tablespoon of the oil in a saucepan and add the onion. Fry gently for 5 minutes until softened.

2 Add the garlic, ginger and spices and fry for a further minute. Add the chopped tomatoes and chillies and cook for another minute.

3 Add the pumpkin and curry paste and fry gently for 3–4 minutes before adding the stock.

4 Stir well, bring to the boil and simmer for 20 minutes until the pumpkin is tender.

5 Thickly slice the banana and add to the pumpkin along with the chickpeas. Simmer for a further 5 minutes.

6 Season to taste with salt and pepper and add the chopped coriander. Serve immediately, garnished with coriander sprigs and some rice or naan bread.

Mediterranean Potato Salad

INGREDIENTS

Serves 4

700 g/1½ lb small waxy potatoes
2 red onions, peeled and
  roughly chopped
1 yellow pepper, deseeded and
  roughly chopped
1 green pepper, deseeded and
  roughly chopped
6 tbsp extra-virgin olive oil
125 g/4 oz ripe tomatoes, chopped
50 g/2 oz pitted black olives, sliced
125 g/4 oz feta cheese
3 tbsp freshly chopped parsley
2 tbsp white wine vinegar
1 tsp Dijon mustard
1 tsp clear honey
salt and freshly ground black pepper
sprigs of fresh parsley, to garnish

1 Preheat the oven to 200°C/400°F/Gas Mark 6. Place the potatoes in a large saucepan of salted water, bring to the boil and simmer until just tender. Do not overcook. Drain and plunge into cold water, to stop them from cooking further.

2 Place the onions in a bowl with the yellow and green peppers, then pour over 2 tablespoons of the olive oil. Stir and spoon onto a large baking tray. Cook in the preheated oven for 25–30 minutes, or until the vegetables are tender and lightly charred in places, stirring occasionally. Remove from the oven and transfer to a large bowl.

3 Cut the potatoes into bite-sized pieces and mix with the roasted onions and peppers. Add the tomatoes and olives to the potatoes. Crumble over the feta cheese and sprinkle with the chopped parsley.

4 Whisk together the remaining olive oil, vinegar, mustard and honey, then season to taste with salt and pepper. Pour the dressing over the potatoes and toss gently together. Garnish with parsley sprigs and serve immediately.

FOOD FACT

Tomatoes are such an integral part of many cuisines, that it is hard to believe they were only introduced to Europe from the Americas a few hundred years ago.

2

3

4

Chinese Steamed Sea Bass with Black Beans

INGREDIENTS

Serves 4

1.1 kg/2½ lb sea bass, cleaned with head and tail left on

1–2 tbsp rice wine or dry sherry

1½ tbsp groundnut oil

2–3 tbsp fermented black beans, rinsed and drained

1 garlic clove, peeled and finely chopped

1 cm/½ inch piece fresh root ginger, peeled and finely chopped

4 spring onions, trimmed and thinly sliced diagonally

2–3 tbsp soy sauce

125 ml/4 fl oz fish or chicken stock

1–2 tbsp sweet Chinese chilli sauce, or to taste

2 tsp sesame oil

sprigs of fresh coriander, to garnish

1 Using a sharp knife, cut 3–4 deep diagonal slashes along both sides of the fish. Sprinkle the Chinese rice wine or sherry inside and over the fish and gently rub into the skin on both sides.

2 Lightly brush a heatproof plate large enough to fit into a large wok or frying pan with a little of the groundnut oil. Place the fish on the plate, curving the fish along the inside edge of the dish, then leave for 20 minutes.

3 Place a wire rack or inverted ramekin in the wok and pour in enough water to come about 2.5 cm/1 inch up the side. Bring to the boil over a high heat.

4 Carefully place the plate with the fish on the rack or ramekin, cover and steam for 12–15 minutes, or until the fish is tender and the flesh is opaque when pierced with a knife near the bone.

5 Remove the plate with the fish from the wok and keep warm. Remove the rack or ramekin from the wok and pour off the water. Return the wok to the heat, add the remaining groundnut oil and swirl to coat the bottom and side. Add the black beans, garlic and ginger and stir-fry for 1 minute.

6 Add the spring onions, soy sauce, fish or chicken stock and boil for 1 minute. Stir in the chilli sauce and sesame oil, then pour the sauce over the cooked fish. Garnish with coriander sprigs and serve immediately.

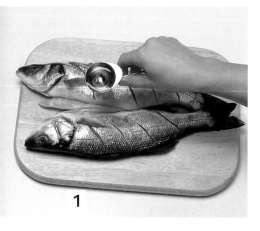

1

2

5

Desserts

Whether catering on a large scale or entertaining close friends you will find something in this collection of desserts to perfectly conclude any occasion. From fruity treats to chocolate indulgence, these recipes will satisfy even the most cultured palate.

Summer Pavlova

INGREDIENTS

Serves 6–8

4 medium egg whites
225 g/8 oz caster sugar
1 tsp vanilla essence
2 tsp white wine vinegar
1½ tsp cornflour
300 ml/½ pint half-fat
  Greek-set yogurt
2 tbsp honey
225 g/8 oz strawberries, hulled
125 g/4 oz raspberries
125 g/4 oz blueberries
4 kiwis, peeled and sliced
icing sugar, to decorate

HELPFUL HINT

Always remember to double check that the bowl being used to whisk egg whites is completely clean, as you will find that any grease will prevent the egg whites from rising into the stiff consistency necessary for this recipe.

1 Preheat the oven to 150°C/300°F/Gas Mark 2. Line a baking sheet with a sheet of greaseproof or baking parchment paper.

2 Place the egg whites in a clean, grease-free bowl and whisk until very stiff.

3 Whisk in half the sugar, vanilla essence, vinegar and cornflour, continue whisking until stiff.

4 Gradually, whisk in the remaining sugar, a teaspoonful at a time until very stiff and glossy.

5 Using a large spoon, arrange spoonfuls of the meringue in a circle on the greaseproof paper or baking parchment paper.

6 Bake in the preheated oven for 1 hour until crisp and dry. Turn the oven off and leave the meringue in the oven to cool completely.

7 Remove the meringue from the baking sheet and peel away the parchment paper. Mix together the yogurt and honey. Place the pavlova on a serving plate and spoon the yogurt into the centre.

8 Scatter over the strawberries, raspberries, blueberries and kiwis. Dust with the icing sugar and serve.

3

5

7

Chocolate Brioche Bake

INGREDIENTS

Serves 6

200 g/7 oz plain dark chocolate,
  broken into pieces
75 g/3 oz unsalted butter
225 g/8 oz brioche, sliced
1 tsp pure orange oil or 1 tbsp grated
  orange rind
½ tsp freshly grated nutmeg
3 medium eggs, beaten
25 g/1 oz golden caster sugar
600 ml/1 pint milk
cocoa powder and icing sugar
  for dusting

1 Preheat the oven to 180°C/350°F/Gas Mark 4, 10 minutes before baking. Lightly oil or butter a 1.7 litre/3 pint ovenproof dish. Melt the chocolate with 25 g/1 oz of the butter in a heatproof bowl set over a saucepan of simmering water. Stir until smooth.

2 Arrange half of the sliced brioche in the ovenproof dish, overlapping the slices slightly, then pour over half of the melted chocolate. Repeat the layers, finishing with a layer of chocolate.

3 Melt the remaining butter in a saucepan. Remove from the heat and stir in the orange oil or rind, the nutmeg and the beaten eggs. Continuing to stir, add the sugar and finally the milk. Beat thoroughly and pour over the brioche. Leave to stand for 30 minutes before baking.

4 Bake on the centre shelf in the preheated oven for 45 minutes, or until the custard is set and the topping is golden brown. Leave to stand for 5 minutes, then dust with cocoa powder and icing sugar. Serve warm.

FOOD FACT

Brioche is a type of French bread, enriched with eggs, butter and sugar. It is available as a large round loaf, as a plait or in a long loaf shape and also as individual buns. Any type is suitable for this recipe.

1

2

3

Crème Brûlée with Sugared Raspberries

INGREDIENTS

Serves 6

600 ml/1 pint fresh whipping cream
4 medium egg yolks
75 g/3 oz caster sugar
½ tsp vanilla essence
25 g/1 oz demerara sugar
175 g/6 oz fresh raspberries

HELPFUL HINT

Most chefs use blow torches to brown the sugar in step 7, as this is the quickest way to caramelise the top of the dessert. Take great care if using a blow torch, especially when lighting. Otherwise use the grill, making sure that it is very hot and the dessert is thoroughly chilled before caramelising the sugar topping. This will prevent the custard underneath from melting.

1 Preheat the oven to 150°C/300°F/Gas Mark 2. Pour the cream into a bowl and place over a saucepan of gently simmering water. Heat gently but do not allow to boil.

2 Meanwhile, whisk together the egg yolks, 50 g/2 oz of the caster sugar and the vanilla essence. When the cream is warm, pour it over the egg mixture briskly whisking until it is mixed completely.

3 Pour into 6 individual ramekin dishes and place in a roasting tin.

4 Fill the tin with sufficient water to come halfway up the sides of the dishes.

5 Bake in the preheated oven for about 1 hour, or until the puddings are set. (To test if set, carefully insert a round bladed knife into the centre, if the knife comes out clean they are set.)

6 Remove the puddings from the roasting tin and allow to cool. Chill in the refrigerator, preferably overnight.

7 Sprinkle the sugar over the top of each dish and place the puddings under a preheated hot grill.

8 When the sugar has caramelised and turned deep brown, remove from the heat and cool. Chill the puddings in the refrigerator for 2–3 hours before serving.

9 Toss the raspberries in the remaining caster sugar and sprinkle over the top of each dish. Serve with a little extra cream if liked.

2

5

7

Raspberry Chocolate Ganache & Berry Tartlets

INGREDIENTS

Serves 8

1 quantity Chocolate Pastry
600 ml/1 pint whipping cream
275 g/10 oz seedless raspberry jam
225 g/8 oz plain dark
   chocolate, chopped
700 g/1½ lb raspberries or other
   summer berries
50 ml/2 fl oz framboise liqueur
1 tbsp caster sugar
crème fraîche, to serve

1 Preheat the oven to 200°C/400°F/Gas Mark 6, 15 minutes before cooking. Make the chocolate pastry and use to line 8 x 7.5 cm/3 inch tartlet tins. Bake blind in the preheated oven for 12 minutes.

2 Place 400 ml/14 fl oz of the cream and half of the raspberry jam in a saucepan and bring to the boil, whisking constantly to dissolve the jam. Remove from the heat and add the chocolate all at once, stirring until the chocolate has melted.

3 Pour into the pastry-lined tartlet tins, shaking gently to distribute the ganache evenly. Chill in the refrigerator for 1 hour or until set.

4 Place the berries in a large shallow bowl. Heat the remaining raspberry jam with half the framboise liqueur over a medium heat until melted and bubbling. Drizzle over the berries and toss gently to coat.

5 Divide the berries among the tartlets, piling them up if necessary. Chill in the refrigerator until ready to serve.

6 Remove the tartlets from the refrigerator for at least 30 minutes before serving. Using an electric whisk, whisk the remaining cream with the caster sugar and the remaining framboise liqueur until it is thick and softly peaking. Serve with the tartlets and crème fraîche.

TASTY TIP

Try substituting an equal quantity of white chocolate for the plain chocolate in this recipe, as raspberries go very well with it.

1

2

3

Black Forest Gateau

INGREDIENTS

Cuts 10–12 slices

250 g/9 oz butter

1 tbsp instant coffee granules

350 ml/12 fl oz hot water

200 g/7 oz plain dark chocolate,
   chopped or broken

400 g/14 oz caster sugar

225 g/8 oz self-raising flour

150 g/5 oz plain flour

50 g/2 oz cocoa powder

2 medium eggs

2 tsp vanilla essence

2 x 400 g cans stoned cherries
   in juice

2 tsp arrowroot

600 ml/1 pint double cream

50 ml/2 fl oz kirsch

HELPFUL HINT

The cake can be assembled and served straightaway but will benefit from being refrigerated for 1–2 hours so that the cream sets slightly. This will make slicing easier.

1 Preheat the oven to 150°C/300°F/Gas Mark 2, 5 minutes before serving. Lightly oil and line a deep 23 cm/9 inch cake tin.

2 Melt the butter. Blend the coffee with the hot water, add to the butter with the chocolate and sugar and heat gently, stirring until smooth. Pour into a large bowl and leave until just warm.

3 Sift together the flours and cocoa powder. Whisk the warm chocolate mixture, then gradually whisk in the dry ingredients. Whisk in the eggs 1 at a time, then the vanilla essence.

4 Pour the mixture into the prepared tin and bake in the preheated oven for 1 hour 45 minutes or until firm. Leave in the tin for 5 minutes to cool slightly before turning out onto a wire rack.

5 Gently heat the cherries and their juice in a small saucepan.

6 Blend the arrowroot with 2 teaspoons of water until smooth, then stir into the cherries. Cook, stirring, until the liquid thickens. Simmer very gently for 2 minutes, then leave until cold.

7 Whisk the double cream until thick. Trim the top of the cake if necessary, then split the cake into 3 layers.

8 Brush the base of the cake with half the kirsch. Top with a layer of cream and one-third of the cherries. Repeat the layering, then place the third layer on top.

9 Reserve a little cream for decorating and use the remainder to cover the top and sides of the cake. Pipe a decorative edge around the cake, then arrange the remaining cherries in the centre and serve.

3

6

7

Italian Polenta Cake with Mascarpone Cream

INGREDIENTS

Cuts into 6–8 slices

1 tsp butter and flour for the tin
100 g/3½ oz plain flour
40 g/1½ oz polenta or
   yellow cornmeal
1 tsp baking powder
¼ tsp salt
grated zest of 1 lemon
2 large eggs
150 g/5 oz caster sugar
5 tbsp milk
½ tsp almond essence
2 tbsp raisins or sultanas
75 g/3 oz unsalted butter, softened
2 medium dessert pears, peeled,
   cored and thinly sliced
2 tbsp apricot jam
175 g/6 oz mascarpone cheese
1–2 tsp sugar
50 ml/2 fl oz double cream
2 tbsp Amaretto liqueur or rum
2–3 tbsp toasted flaked almonds
icing sugar, to dust

1 Preheat the oven to 190°C/375°F/Gas Mark 5 10 minutes before baking. Butter a 23 cm/9 inch springform tin. Dust lightly with flour.

2 Stir the flour, polenta or cornmeal, baking powder, salt and lemon zest together. Beat the eggs and half the sugar until light and fluffy. Slowly beat in the milk and almond essence.

3 Stir in the raisins or sultanas, then beat in the flour mixture and 50 g/2 oz of the butter.

4 Spoon into the tin and smooth the top evenly. Arrange the pear slices on top in overlapping concentric circles.

5 Melt the remaining butter and brush over the pear slices. Sprinkle with the rest of the sugar.

6 Bake in the preheated oven for about 40 minutes, until puffed and golden and the edges of the pears are lightly caramelised. Transfer to a wire rack. Reserve to cool in the tin for 15 minutes.

7 Remove the cake from the tin. Heat the apricot jam with 1 tablespoon of water and brush over the top of the cake to glaze.

8 Beat the mascarpone cheese with the sugar to taste, the cream and Amaretto or rum until smooth and forming a soft dropping consistency. Serve with the polenta cake.

9 When cool, sprinkle the almonds over the polenta cake and dust generously with the icing sugar. Serve the cake with the liqueur-flavoured mascarpone cream on the side.

1

4

7

Coconut Rice Served with Stewed Ginger Fruits

INGREDIENTS

Serves 6–8

1 vanilla pod
450 ml/³⁄₄ pint coconut milk
1.1 litres/2 pints semi-skimmed milk
600 ml/1 pint double cream
100 g/3½ oz caster sugar
2 star anise
8 tbsp toasted desiccated coconut
250 g/9 oz short-grain pudding rice
1 tsp melted butter
2 mandarin oranges, peeled and
  pith removed
1 star fruit, sliced
50 g/2 oz stem ginger, finely diced
300 ml/½ pint sweet white wine
caster sugar, to taste

FOOD FACT

Star fruit is a pale yellow-green fruit with a pretty star-shaped appearance when cut horizontally. It is almost flavourless with just a hint of sweet and sour and has a crunchy texture when eaten raw. Poaching it in white wine and ginger makes it taste as good as it looks.

1 Preheat the oven to 160°C/325°F/Gas Mark 3. Using a sharp knife, split the vanilla pod in half lengthways, scrape out the seeds from the pods and place both the pod and seeds in a large heavy-based casserole dish. Pour in the coconut milk, the semi-skimmed milk and the double cream and stir in the sugar, star anise and 4 tablespoons of the toasted coconut. Bring to the boil, then simmer for 10 minutes, stirring occasionally. Remove the vanilla pod and star anise.

2 Wash the rice and add to the milk. Simmer gently for 25–30 minutes or until the rice is tender, stirring frequently. Stir in the melted butter.

3 Divide the mandarins into segments and place in a saucepan with the sliced star fruit and stem ginger. Pour in the white wine and 300 ml/½ pint water, bring to the boil, then reduce the heat and simmer for 20 minutes or until the liquid has reduced and the fruits softened. Add sugar to taste.

4 Serve the rice, topped with the stewed fruits and the remaining toasted coconut.

Ricotta Cheesecake with Strawberry Coulis

INGREDIENTS

Serves 6–8

125 g/4 oz digestive biscuits
100 g/3½ oz candied peel, chopped
65 g/2½ oz butter, melted
150 ml/¼ pint crème fraîche
575 g/4 oz ricotta cheese
100 g/3½ oz caster sugar
1 vanilla pod, seeds only
2 large eggs
225 g/8 oz strawberries
25–50 g/1–2 oz caster sugar, to taste
zest and juice of 1 orange

TASTY TIP

This cheesecake has a soft, creamy texture compared to some baked cheesecakes. This is because of the addition of crème fraîche. If ricotta is unavailable, substitute with full-fat soft cheese.

1　Preheat oven to 170°C/325°F/Gas Mark 3. Line a 20.5 cm/8 inch springform tin with baking parchment. Place the biscuits into a food processor together with the peel. Blend until the biscuits are crushed and the peel is chopped. Add 50 g/2 oz of the melted butter and process until mixed. Tip into the tin and spread evenly over the bottom. Press firmly into place and reserve.

2　Blend together the crème fraîche, ricotta cheese, sugar, vanilla seeds and eggs in a food processor. With the motor running, add the remaining melted butter and blend for a few seconds. Pour the mixture on to the base. Transfer to the preheated oven and cook for about 1 hour, until set and risen round the edges, but slightly wobbly in the centre. Switch off the oven and allow to cool there. Chill in the refrigerator for at least 8 hours, preferably overnight.

3　Wash and drain the strawberries. Hull the fruit and remove any soft spots. Put into the food processor along with 25 g/1 oz of the sugar and orange juice and zest. Blend until smooth. Add the remaining sugar to taste. Pass through a sieve to remove seeds and chill in the refrigerator until needed.

4　Cut the cheesecake into wedges, spoon over some of the strawberry coulis and serve.

1

2

3

Almond & Pistachio Biscotti

INGREDIENTS

Makes 12 biscuits

125 g/4 oz ground almonds
50 g/2 oz shelled pistachios
50 g/2 oz blanched almonds
2 medium eggs
1 medium egg yolk
125 g/4 oz icing sugar
225 g/8 oz plain flour
1 tsp baking powder
pinch of salt
zest of ½ lemon

1 Preheat oven to 180°C/350°F/Gas Mark 4. Line a large baking sheet with non-stick baking parchment. Toast the ground almonds and whole nuts lightly and reserve until cool.

2 Beat together the eggs, egg yolk and icing sugar until thick, then beat in the flour, baking powder and salt. Add the lemon zest, ground almonds and whole nuts and mix to form a slightly sticky dough.

3 Turn the dough on to a lightly floured surface and, using lightly floured hands, form into a log measuring approximately 30 cm/ 12 inches long. Place down the centre of the prepared baking sheet and transfer to the preheated oven. Bake for 20 minutes.

4 Remove from the oven and increase the oven temperature to 200°C/400°F/Gas Mark 6. Cut the log diagonally into 2.5 cm/1 inch slices. Return to the baking sheet, cut-side down, and bake for a further 10–15 minutes until golden, turning once after 10 minutes. Leave to cool on a wire rack and store in an airtight container.

TASTY TIP

These biscuits are also delicious made with a single kind of nut – try hazelnuts or just almonds. When toasting nuts spread them out on a baking sheet then place in a preheated oven at 200°C/ 400°F/Gas Mark 6. Leave for 5–10 minutes, stirring occasionally. If using a lower temperature, leave for a few more minutes.

1

2

4

Bomba Siciliana

INGREDIENTS

Serves 6–8

100 g/3½ oz plain chocolate, broken
  into pieces
200 g/7 oz fresh chilled custard
150 ml/¼ pint whipping cream
25 g/1 oz candied peel,
  finely chopped
25 g/1 oz glacé cherries, chopped
25 g/1 oz sultanas
3 tbsp rum
225 g/8 oz good quality
  vanilla ice cream
200 ml/¼ pint double cream
3 tbsp caster sugar

TASTY TIP

For the best flavour, buy whole candied peel. Cut it into strips using kitchen scissors, then chop crosswise into small pieces.

1 Melt the plain chocolate in bowl set over a saucepan of simmering water until smooth, then cool. Whisk together the custard with the whipping cream and slightly cooled chocolate. Spoon the mixture into a shallow, lidded freezer box and freeze. Every 2 hours, remove from the freezer and, using an electric whisk or balloon whisk, whisk thoroughly. Repeat 3 times, then leave until frozen solid. Soak the candied peel, cherries and sultanas in the rum and leave until needed.

2 Chill a bombe or 1 litre/1¾ pint pudding mould in the freezer for about 30 minutes. Remove the chocolate ice cream from the freezer to soften, then spoon the ice cream into the mould and press down well, smoothing around the edges and leaving a hollow in the centre. Return the ice cream to the freezer for about 1 hour, or until frozen hard.

3 Remove the vanilla ice cream from the freezer to soften. Spoon the softened vanilla ice cream into the hollow, making sure to leave another hollow for the cream. Return to the freezer again and freeze until hard.

4 Whip the cream and sugar until it is just holding its shape then fold in the soaked fruit. Remove the mould from the freezer and spoon in the cream mixture. Return to the freezer for at least another hour.

5 When ready to serve, remove the mould from the freezer and dip into hot water for a few seconds, then turn on to a large serving plate. Dip a knife into hot water and cut into wedges to serve.

1

1

2

Zabaglione with Rum–soaked Raisin Compote

INGREDIENTS

Serves 6

2 tbsp raisins

1 strip thinly pared lemon zest

½ tsp ground cinnamon

3 tbsp Marsala wine

3 medium egg yolks

3 tbsp caster sugar

125 ml/4 fl oz dry white wine

150 ml/¼ pint double cream,
  lightly whipped

crisp biscuits, to serve

1 Put the raisins in a small bowl with the lemon zest and ground cinnamon. Pour over the Marsala wine to cover and leave to macerate for at least one hour. When the raisins are plump, lift out of the Marsala wine and reserve the raisins and wine, discarding the lemon zest.

2 In a large heatproof bowl, mix together the egg yolks and sugar. Add the white wine and Marsala wine and stir well to combine. Put the bowl over a saucepan of simmering water, ensuring that the bottom of the bowl does not touch the water. Whisk constantly until the mixture doubles in bulk.

3 Remove from the heat and continue whisking for about 5 minutes until the mixture has cooled slightly. Fold in the raisins and then immediately fold in the whipped cream. Spoon into dessert glasses or goblets and serve with crisp biscuits.

FOOD FACT

Zabaglione, an Italian concoction of eggs, sugar and wine, is virtually identical to Sabayon – a French concoction of eggs, sugar and wine. Make the zabaglione as above and omit the raisins. Serve with poached pears, summer fruits or on its own in stemmed glasses.

1

2

3

Tiramisu

INGREDIENTS

Serves 4

225 g/8 oz mascarpone cheese
25 g/1 oz icing sugar, sifted
150 ml/¼ pint strong brewed
  coffee, chilled
300 ml/½ pint double cream
3 tbsp coffee liqueur
125 g/4 oz Savoiardi or sponge
  finger biscuits
50 g/2 oz plain dark chocolate, grated
  or made into small curls
cocoa powder, for dusting
assorted summer berries, to serve

1 Lightly oil and line a 900 g/2 lb loaf tin with a piece of clingfilm. Put the mascarpone cheese and icing sugar into a large bowl and using a rubber spatula, beat until smooth. Stir in 2 tablespoons of chilled coffee and mix thoroughly.

2 Whip the cream with 1 tablespoon of the coffee liqueur until just thickened. Stir a spoonful of the whipped cream into the mascarpone mixture, then fold in the rest. Spoon half of the the mascarpone mixture into the prepared loaf tin and smooth the top.

3 Put the remaining coffee and coffee liqueur into a shallow dish just bigger than the biscuits. Using half of the biscuits, dip one side of each biscuit into the coffee mixture, then arrange on top of the mascarpone mixture in a single layer. Spoon the rest of the mascarpone mixture over the biscuits and smooth the top.

4 Dip the remaining biscuits in the coffee mixture and arrange on top of the mascarpone mixture. Drizzle with any remaining coffee mixture. Cover with clingfilm and chill in the refrigerator for 4 hours.

5 Carefully turn the tiramisu out on to a large serving plate and sprinkle with the grated chocolate or chocolate curls. Dust with cocoa powder, cut into slices and serve with a few summer berries.

FOOD FACT

This now classic Italian dessert appears in all kinds of forms in most Italian cookery books. The name literally means 'pick me up'.

1

2

3

Crunchy Rhubarb Crumble

INGREDIENTS

Serves 6

125 g/4 oz plain flour
50 g/2 oz softened butter
50 g/2 oz rolled oats
50 g/2 oz demerara sugar
1 tbsp sesame seeds
½ tsp ground cinnamon
450 g/1 lb fresh rhubarb
50 g/2 oz caster sugar
custard or cream, to serve

TASTY TIP

To make homemade custard, pour 600 ml/1 pint of milk with a few drops of vanilla essence into a saucepan and bring to the boil. Remove from the heat and allow to cool. Meanwhile, whisk 5 egg yolks and 3 tablespoons of caster sugar together in a mixing bowl until thick and pale in colour. Add the milk, stir and strain into a heavy-based saucepan. Cook the custard on a low heat, stirring constantly until the consistency of double cream. Pour over the rhubarb crumble and serve.

1 Preheat the oven to 180°C/350°F/Gas Mark 4. Place the flour in a large bowl and cut the butter into cubes. Add to the flour and rub in with the fingertips until the mixture looks like fine breadcrumbs, or blend for a few seconds in a food processor.

2 Stir in the rolled oats, demerara sugar, sesame seeds and cinnamon. Mix well and reserve.

3 Prepare the rhubarb by removing the thick ends of the stalks and cut diagonally into 2.5 cm/1 inch chunks. Wash thoroughly and pat dry with a clean tea towel. Place the rhubarb in a 1.1 litre/2 pint pie dish.

4 Sprinkle the caster sugar over the rhubarb and top with the reserved crumble mixture. Level the top of the crumble so that all the fruit is well covered and press down firmly. If liked, sprinkle the top with a little extra caster sugar.

5 Place on a baking sheet and bake in the preheated oven for 40–50 minutes, or until the fruit is soft and the topping is golden brown. Sprinkle the pudding with some more caster sugar and serve hot with custard or cream.

2

3

4

Iced Bakewell Tart

INGREDIENTS

Cuts into 8 slices

For the rich pastry:
175 g/6 oz plain flour
pinch of salt
60 g/2½ oz butter, cut into
  small pieces
50 g/2 oz white vegetable fat,
  cut into small pieces
2 small egg yolks, beaten

For the filling:
125 g/4 oz butter, melted
125 g/4 oz caster sugar
125 g/4 oz ground almonds
2 large eggs, beaten
few drops of almond essence
2 tbsp seedless raspberry jam

For the icing:
125 g/4 oz icing sugar, sifted
6–8 tsp fresh lemon juice
25 g/1 oz toasted flaked almonds

1 Preheat the oven to 200°C/400°F/Gas Mark 6. Place the flour and salt in a bowl, rub in the butter and vegetable fat until the mixture resembles breadcrumbs. Alternatively, blend quickly, in short bursts in a food processor.

2 Add the eggs with sufficient water to make a soft, pliable dough. Knead lightly on a floured board then chill in the refrigerator for about 30 minutes. Roll out the pastry and use to line a 23 cm/9 inch loose-bottomed flan tin.

3 For the filling, mix together the melted butter, sugar, almonds and beaten eggs and add a few drops of almond essence. Spread the base of the pastry case with the raspberry jam and spoon over the egg mixture.

4 Bake in the preheated oven for about 30 minutes, or until the filling is firm and golden brown. Remove from the oven and allow to cool completely.

5 When the tart is cold make the icing by mixing together the icing sugar and lemon juice, a little at a time, until the icing is smooth and of a spreadable consistency.

6 Spread the icing over the tart, leave to set for 2–3 minutes and sprinkle with the almonds. Chill in the refrigerator for about 10 minutes and serve.

2

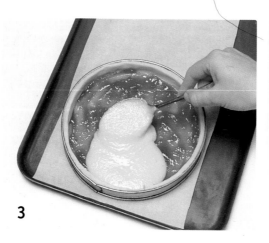

3

6

Chocolate Profiteroles

INGREDIENTS

Serves 4

For the pastry:

150 ml/¼ pint water

50 g/2 oz butter

65 g/2½ oz plain flour, sifted

2 medium eggs, lightly beaten

For the custard:

300 ml/½ pint milk

pinch of freshly grated nutmeg

3 medium egg yolks

50 g/2 oz caster sugar

2 tbsp plain flour, sifted

2 tbsp cornflour, sifted

For the sauce:

175 g/6 oz soft brown sugar

150 ml/¼ pint boiling water

1 tsp instant coffee

1 tbsp cocoa powder

1 tbsp brandy

75 g/3 oz butter

1 tbsp golden syrup

1 Preheat the oven to 220°C/425°F/Gas Mark 7, 15 minutes before cooking. Lightly oil 2 baking sheets. For the pastry, place the water and the butter in a heavy-based saucepan and bring to the boil. Remove from the heat and beat in the flour. Return to the heat and cook for 1 minute or until the mixture forms a ball in the centre of the saucepan.

2 Remove from the heat and leave to cool slightly, then gradually beat in the eggs a little at a time, beating well after each addition. Once all the eggs have been added, beat until the paste is smooth and glossy. Pipe or spoon 20 small balls onto the baking sheets, allowing plenty of room for expansion.

3 Bake in the preheated oven for 25 minutes or until well risen and golden brown. Reduce the oven temperature to 180°C/350°F/Gas Mark 4. Make a hole in each ball and continue to bake for a further 5 minutes. Remove from the oven and leave to cool.

4 For the custard, place the milk and nutmeg in a heavy-based saucepan and bring to the boil. In another saucepan, whisk together the egg yolks, sugar and the flours, then beat in the hot milk. Bring to the boil and simmer, whisking constantly for 2 minutes. Cover and leave to cool.

5 Spoon the custard into the profiteroles and arrange on a large serving dish. Place all the sauce ingredients in a small saucepan and bring to the boil, then simmer for 10 minutes. Remove from the heat and cool slightly before serving with the chocolate profiteroles.

1

2

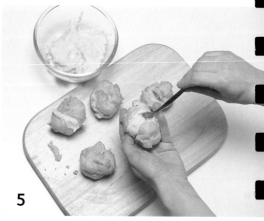

5

Index